# Akhenaten
# Egypt's Mysterious Pharaoh

## Travis "T.J." Frank

# Contents

*For Akhenaten,*

*Thank You*

'

*Beautifully you appear from the horizon of heaven, O Living Aten who initiates life- For you are risen from the eastern and have filled every land with your beauty; For you are fair, great, dazzling, and high over every land, and your rays enclose the lands to the limits of all you have made...'*

- *'The Great Hymn to the Aten'*

# 1

# A Monumental Discovery

It's the year 1887, a Bedouin woman from the village of Tell el-Amarna is hastily digging in the sands. What could she be looking for? Is she a worker digging up forgotten artifacts lost to the sands of time? Or is she is digging up treasure for herself? Not exactly. This Bedouin is in fact looking for a dried mud brick called *sebakh*. Sebakh, rich in phosphates, was highly sought after by the Bedouins as fertilizer for their fields; however, large quantities of sebakh could only be found in ancient structures. Luckily for the Bedouin woman, the site she happened to be digging at was home to an ancient city known throughout the centuries to be "cursed".

Centuries prior, ancient Beni-Amran had settled in this area of Egypt known to the ancient Egyptians as Middle Egypt. Once settled in their new homes, the Beni-Amran established four villages: *el-Till, el-Hagg Qandil, el-Amiriya*, and *el-Hawata*. By combining the names of the tribes produces a new name; in the case of the Bedouin woman she was a member of the el-Till el-Amarna tribe. Despite Amarna's reputation as a cursed

site, didn't stop the Beni-Amran from settling and cultivating free land; let alone dig at the village's ancient structures. As the Bedouin continued her quest to find sebakh, she hears a loud "clink". Success! Overjoyed, the Bedouin woman hastily tossed her spade to the side and plunged her hands into the hot sands to claim her prize, but when she pulled out her prize, her enthusiasm turned into confusion.

She glanced the strange rectangular shape clay in her hands.; it looked no bigger than an average dog biscuit and as she turned it around there appeared strange wedge-shaped markings. Although not the sebakh, the Bedouin woman tossed the clay biscuit into her basket, picked up her spade and resumed her quest. The Bedouin woman continued to dig under the unforgiving heat-which must've felt like hours than minutes- and no less than five minutes did her spade contact something. She once again tossed her spade to the side and plunged her hands into the hot sands only to be disappointed again when she pulled another biscuit-shaped clay with the same wedged-shaped markings.

Cursing to herself, she grabbed her spade and basket and moved to another spot. Surely, a new spot would yield sebakh right? Despite renewed determination, the Bedouin woman began digging, and digging, until she discovered not one, but exactly three hundred and sixty biscuit shaped clays with the wedge-shaped markings! Now she was fuming. She had been up early in the morning- to dodge the rising heat-looking for sebakh and all her backbreaking work yielded worthless clay!

Sobbing, she wearily picked herself up from the sands-her body feeling like lead- and placed all the worthless clays into a

sack. As she was about to leave for home, the Bedouin woman stopped halfway. She felt an itch at the back of her head that she couldn't quite scratch. She remembered there were "foreigners" digging all around Egypt looking for worthless junk; however, she heard how these foreigners not only got excited when they discovered this junk but how much they pay for it. Her lips began curling into a sinister smile; perhaps all that backbreaking work was worth it in the end. She took a glance into her sack and shook the dust covered clays and quickly dashed back to the village.

By the time she returned to the village, the Bedouin woman desperately looked for one of these foreigners to sell her sack of meaningless clay for much needed money. But as she was looking for a buyer, the Bedouin woman ran into her neighbor. She shows her neighbor the sack full of the biscuit shaped clays and recounts her ordeal to the neighbor of failing to unearth sebakh, only to dig up these biscuit shaped clays with strange markings and was looking for a buyer to sell them off to.

The neighbor, seizing the opportunity of a lifetime, cunningly convinced the Bedouin woman to sell him the sack full of clays for ten piastres (less than ten cents). Looking to the piastres and back to the sack, the Bedouin handed the neighbor the sack containing the biscuit shaped clays and flew off with her newfound wealth. As far as history goes, the Bedouin woman was never mentioned again; however, this was just the beginning of what would become a discovery of a lifetime.

## A New Discovery, but a New Mystery

After deceptively swindling the Bedouin woman of her clays, the neighbor took off to find one of these foreigners to sell to for

**One of the dog biscuit shaped clay's with the strange wedge-shaped markings discovered by the Bedouin woman in 1887.**

a big pay day. Eventually, the neighbor stumbles upon an antiques dealer and presents him the dust covered biscuit clays. Intrigued by their size, shape, and markings, the dealer asked the Bedouin the location to where he found the tablets. Once disclosing the location to where he "found them," the dealer bought the clays off the neighbor for a hefty sum.

Later that day, the dealer took another look at the biscuit shaped clays and decided to examine them more thoroughly. At first, he wasn't sure what these markings could be, but after hours of backtracking, he was shocked to discover these weren't ordinary markings- they were a written language not native to Egypt. This written language, Akkadian, was used by

**Ancient cuneiform piece from Mesopotamia**

the ancient Mesopotamian's- commonly referred to as
Cuneiform due to the wedge-shaped markings and could be
found on *Cuneiform Tablets*- but how why were tablets
containing Mesopotamian dialect doing in Egypt? And more
importantly, why were they discovered at this one site? Limited
by his knowledge of the cuneiform tablets, the dealer sent them
back to Europe to get a second opinion on their validity.

Soon after their arrival to Europe, the cuneiform tablets made
their way to Europe's prestige museums. Many renowned
linguists, scholars, and historians observed the tablets and
although they agree they are cuneiform, they doubted if these
were genuine. There those who believed these tablets were

genuine while others scoffed it off as an elaborate hoax from the locals to get rich, but how would a Bedouin know how to create, let alone, read, and write in Akkadian?

To settle this dispute once and for all, the curator of the British Museum tasked a man named **Ernest Alfred Wallis Budge** to go to Egypt and discover more of the tablets. Budge was the perfect choice for the British Museum to send off to Egypt. He was the head of the museum's Department of Egyptian and Assyrian Antiquities and was an expert in the Akkadian language. Budge had heard the rumors going around the academic community of more cuneiform tablets in Egypt, but as he sailed off for Egypt, finding these tablets would prove to be a more dangerous task then he bargained for.

## Quest for the Cuneiform Tablets

Around the time the dealer had discovered the cuneiform tablets, the Cairo Museum's Antiquities Department began cracking down on the illegal selling and smuggling of ancient artifacts to private collectors. Under the department's official, **Monsieur Grebaut**, issued a decree throughout Egypt: those who are in possession or selling of these tablets would be thrown to jail. To make matters worse, those who had any connection to someone who had seen the tablets or had one, were sent to jail as well.

For the dealers, they weren't going to give up what could be a large payday; however, they didn't want to go to jail for having them either. When questioned by Grebaut, the dealers would lie and act as if they only head about the discovery, but these dealers were sent to jail regardless. How did Grebaut knew these dealers were lying? Unbeknownst to the general populace, Grebaut had a small network of spies all over Egypt.

These spies acted as Grebaut's eyes and ears who reported to Grebaut on the whereabouts of the tablets and the dealers who where in possession of selling them off. Those who got off with a stern warning were the lucky ones. Anyone caught in their lie and deceit would be tortured until they told the truth. This was the fate for Budge if he wished to look for the tablets. From the moment he stepped onto Egyptian soil, Budge was already being eyed by Grebaut's spies.

When word came back from his spies of Budge's arrival and meetings with the local dealers, Grebaut knew Budge was here to buy the tablets for his benefactor and greedily smuggle them back to Europe. Grebaut ordered his spies to shadow Budge's movements and report to him daily of his meetings with the dealers and his whereabouts. This proved to be more troubling for the local dealers. Any dealer caught discussing the tablets with Budge were arrested, prosecuted, and tortured. For their safety, some of the dealers refused to discuss- let alone meet Budge in person- about the tablets.

It was during his stay at Luxor when Budge received a special message from a secret messenger. The messenger warned Budge that he has been sticking his nose where it shouldn't be over the tablets and Grebaut-with a warrant- was coming to Luxor to personally arrest Budge. When Budge inquired to how long he had to leave before Greabaut could arrest him, the messenger- with a giddy smirk- informs Budge Grebaut would be running late. Perplexed by the messenger's vague response, Budge demanded why Greabut would be running late. The messenger-to ease Budge's anxiety- recounts the story he had heard from the locals. According to the messenger's story, Grebaut was indeed on his way to Luxor and decided the fastest way to get there was by taking a steamer.

**Ernest Alfred Wallis Budge circa. 1920**

When the steamer was going too slow, Grebaut ordered the
captain to make the steamer not only go faster but do not stop
at any town or village- which made the captain rightfully angry
and upset since it was his daughter's wedding day.

As the steamer was making good timing, the steamer suddenly
crashed into a sands bar. Whether it was fate or luck, the
combined might of the crew couldn't pry the steamer off the
sands bar. Enraged knowing his opening to catch Budge was
slipping from his fingertips, Greabut stormed off to the
countryside. There, he demanded the villagers to commandeer
one of their donkeys- to make the twelve-mile journey to

Luxor- and threatened those who didn't follow his orders were
to be arrested and sent to jail, but in a twist Grebaut didn't

~ 13 ~

expect, there was no donkey to be found in the village. Word had gotten out of Grebaut's threats of imprisoning those who refused to give him a donkey and after living in fear of this man, decided to have some fun by making his trip as miserable as possible.

They did this by taking every donkey and drove them off to the fields. Budge could now breathe in a sigh of relief knowing he would be long gone before Grebaut could catch him and his spies wouldn't be able to communicate with their master. All Budge had to do was now wait for the local dealer who was in possession of the tablets and see if these tablets were the genuine deal or not.

## The Amarna Letters

While he was waiting for the dealer to deliver him the tablets, Budge decided to treat himself with a nice cup of coffee at the local café. By the time he finished his first cup, the dealer arrived bearing Budge a gift: six new cuneiform tablets. From there, Budge-with his notepad and pen in hand- began his observation of the tablets. Throughout his observations, Budge, like others within the academic community, too began to doubt the validity of the tablets. They seemed too perfect as if they were just recently cut and marked. In his notes, Budge recounts the ordeal he had over deciding if these tablets were either *kadim* (old) or *jaded* (new):

**The ancient ruins at Amarna**

"When I examined the tablets, I found that the matter was not as simple as it looked. In shape and form, and colour and material, the tablets were unlike any I had ever seen in London or Paris; and this writing on all of them was of a most unusual character and puzzled me for hours."

Although he was puzzled by the tablet's authenticity at first, Budge still believed these tablets held great historical importance. Once he concluded his research, Budge bought the six tablets from the dealer and took them back to the British Museum where they currently reside today. Indeed, Budge's

**(Top/Bottom) Collection of Amarna Letters**

recovery of the six cuneiform tablets was accepted by the academic community not only historically important but a monumental one. According to his observations, these weren't ordinary cuneiform tablets, they were in fact written letters between the pharaoh and the king and an Eastern king from the Kingdom of Mitanni. What the Bedouin woman had stumbled upon was the remnants of the ancient world's largest caches of diplomatic letters between Egypt and the Near East. "They would provide a remarkable insight into [Egyptian] civilization in general and diplomacy in particular of Ancient Near East."

These tablets, moving forward, would be referred to as the **Amarna Letters**-named after where they were first discovered at the village of Tell el-Amarna. According to scholars, they dated the Amarna Letters from 1355-1330 BC, spanning over the reign of two pharaohs; the first being the 'Dazzling Orb' **Amenhotep III** and a pharaoh-whom many scholars barely knew existed due to the lack of evidence-that would go down in history as Egypt's heretical king, his name was **Akhenaten.**

# 2

# Rebirth of The Sun Pharaoh

When Budge reported his translated to the British Museum about the mysterious Akhenaten, many were intrigued of the discovery of a previously unknown pharaoh. Who was he? What did he look like? Why didn't archaeologists discover any sculptures or reliefs of Akhenaten? And why was his name found at the village of Amarna and not in Thebes? These kinds of questions plagued Egyptologists, scholars, and historians alike. This discovery proved to both the academic and archaeological institutions there maybe more to Amarna than previously thought. But this wasn't their first time hearing about Akhenaten and the Amarna ruins. In fact, the ruins of Amarna had not only been known for nearly a century, but the name of Akhenaten was hinted for at least forty years before the discovery of the Amarna letters.

For centuries, the ruins at Amarna had been nearly forgotten by Egypt. Seen only as a cursed site, the ruins laid undisturbed until the year 1714, when a Jesuit explorer named **Claude Sicard** became the first outsider in three thousand years to gander at the ruins. As he was traveling Egypt, Sicard came upon the site of *Tuna el-Gebel*. In his journal, Sicard describes a massive stele-surrounded by figures on both sides- cut deeply into the mountainside. At the time, Sicard didn't know the significance of his find, but what he discovered would prove to be beneficial to unlocking the forgotten history of Akhenaten.

## The First Expedition at Amarna

In 1798, French forces under general **Napoleon Bonaparte**, landed his troops on the sands of Egypt did the first record of Amarna's ruins come into the minds of Europeans. Napoleon had landed in Egypt with the main goal to gain full control of a new trade route to India via the Isthmus of Suez (modern Suez Canal), but before his departure, Napoleon enlisted artisans, translators, and scholars to accompany him to Egypt.

 With the task to record and translate Egypt's ancient and modern histories. Between 1798-1799, Napoleon's rag tag band swept across Egypt making drawings of Egypt's ancient wonders, decrepit and fallen statues, and recording the hieroglyphs plastered on every wall on every monument and temple. This was to be known as the famous Napoleon Expedition. It would be during this grueling two-year expedition when Bonaparte's men stumbled across the ruins of Amarna. Seeing the ruins sticking out from the sands left a profound mark on French surveyor **Edme' Jomard**:

'I was surprised to see a great mass of ruins…no less than
two thousand metres long and a thousand miles wide, yet
which, though situated near the Nile…. However, one    still
finds a very great number of houses in brick with
with their principal walls, a large gateway, and enclosure.'

**Portrait sketch of Edme' Jomard**

At the time, Jomard and the French knew nothing of the ruin's importance to Egypt's lengthy history, but all their hard work wouldn't go to waste. Jomard and his team drew and recorded what ruins were visible, but their work would be sidelined in **Dominique Denon's** *Description de l'Egypte*- one of the world's first books on Egyptology- in favor of the more well-known pyramids and Sphinx.

## Other Expeditions at Amarna

Despite Jomard and his team's efforts at Amarna, no European had their sights visiting the ruins anytime soon; until 1824, when English traveler, **John Gardner Wilkinson** discovered the tombs of Akhenaten's royal officials deep within the mountainside. At the time, Wilkinson couldn't read the hieroglyphs on the tomb walls, yet he was an artist and decided to sketch and record the tomb wall reliefs. The next time a European entered Amarna would be four years later, in 1828 when renowned French linguist, **Jean Francios Champollion**-the decipherer of the hieroglyphics and father of modern Egyptology- lead a grueling sixteen-month journey into the heart of Egypt to record; to unlock the meanings of the hieroglyphics.

It was in November 1828, when Champollion made his way to the ruins of Amarna and after spending an entire day-he was on the move for much of his time there- recorded in his note's figures standing on opposite ends of a large boundary stele. "King very fat and swollen, big belly. Feminine contours...grande morbidezilla [considerable softness]." Although Champollion didn't find Akhenaten's name, he indirectly gave the first physical description to what Akhenaten may have looked like, yet he wasn't sure if the figure he gazed at was masculine or feminine due to the amalgamation of the two.

## Lepsius: Discoverer of Akhenaten

On September 19th, 1843, under Prussian King Fredrich Wilhelm IV, **Karl Richard Lepsius** led the very first lengthy expedition at Amarna, but not the ruins. At first, Lepsius theorized the strange figure (Akhenaten) was not a male pharaoh but a woman taking upon the role as pharaoh. On November 20, 1843, Lepsius sent a letter to colleague where he deduced the figure on the walls was indeed a man and was called '*Bec-en-Aten*'. By this point, it was theorized

Akhenaten-before his finding his name- was feminine but Lepsius put those theories to rest. He concluded the figure was a man and this pharaoh had a name to go with it. On June 26th , 1851, Lepsius presented his work to the Prussian Academy of Sciences called work to the Prussian Academy of Scieneces called *On the Earliest Pantheon and ist Historical and Mythological Origin*; where he describes 'Bec-en-Aten' who opposed the cult of Amun-Ra in favor of a cult dedicated to solar worship":

> 'Through the monuments we became acquainted with several kings of this period [the 18th Dynasty], who were not afterwards admitted in the legitmate lists, but were regarded as unauthorized co-temporary or intermediate kings. Among these Amenophis IV, is to be particularly noted, who, during a very active reign of twelve [sic] years endeavoured to accomplish a complete reformation of all secular and spiritual instituitons. He built a royal capital for himself in Central Egypt, near the present Tel el-Amarna, introduced new offices and useages, and aimed at no less a thing than than to abolish the whole religious system of the Egyptians, which had hitherto subsisted, and to place in its stead the single worship of the Sun....Indeed, the former gods and their worship were persecuted to such an extent by this king, that he erased all the god's names with the single execption of the Sun-god Ra, from every monument that was accesible throughout the country, and because his own name, Amenophis, contained the name Ammon [Amun], he changed it to Bec-en-Aten [Akhenaten], "Worshipper of the Sun Disc"....'

Among those who were present at Lepsius' findings were intrigued by how this Bec-en-Aten singlehandidly overthrew centuries of tradition in favor of a solar disc. They further noted the name of Bec-en-Aten was etched out from historical record, yet his name was found in this one area. It seemed to Lepsius that this radical ideological change by Bec-en-Aten wasn't universally praised by the Egyptians and erased him from their own history to cover up this tumultous time.

## The First Scientific Excavation at Amarna

Despite Lepsius incredible findings at Amarna of the mysterious Bec-en-Aten-and providing a forgotten story in Egypt's history- there would be no further excavations at Amarna. It's unclear why archaeologists decided to abandon any interest in Amarna for several decades- after Lepsius treasure drove of evidence- but that didn't stop the site from becoming active again. In the 1880's, Bedouins had stumbled upon a massive room cut deep into Amarna's eastern side cliffs that reinvigorated the academic community to take an interest in Amarna again.

For some time, the Bedouins kept the discovery a secret from the foreigners; however, when the tomb was successfully excavated, it proved to be the tomb of Akhenaten. Between 1891-1892 Further work in the tomb would be led by **Alessandro Barsanti**, but most of his work would be lost. In 1891, archaeologist, **William Flinder's Petrie**, was chosen by the *EEF* (*Egypt Exploration Fund*) to lead a new scientific excavation of Amarna's ruins.

Petrie is regarded today as the founder of modern archaeology- and correctly measured the Great Pyramid of Khufu that's still

Portrait of Karl Richard Lepsius 1850

**Sketch from the Lepsius Project. 19th Century**

used as the golden standard in pyramid measurement- due to his methodical scientific process of excavation. He believed everything should be recorded in detail from wall reliefs to mundane items such as pottery- where he would receive the nickname *'Father of Pots'*- and every discovery should be treated with the utmost respect and care; so future generations can appreciate and be inspired by the ancient wonders of the past.

Amongst those who worked under Petrie was a young seventeen-year-old artist named **Howard Carter;** who would go on-inspired by Petrie's methods- to become an excavator himself. Carter's life would be linked with Akhenaten's when, 30 years after he left Amarna, discovered the tomb of Tutankhamun on November 22, 1922.

What drew Petrie to Amarna wasn't the *Amarna Letters* first discovered by the Bedouin woman, not the tombs or Akhenaten- like Lepsius or Basranti were drawn to- it was the prospect of working on a site that wasn't damaged by other treasure hunters. Petrie first began excavating where the Bedouin woman had found the Amarna Letters the first time.

Here, Petrie discovered what appeared to be a *Foreign Office*- an ancient equivalent to the modern postal service- where incoming cuneiform tablets were received by Egypt's allies and vassal states; with scribes writing outgoing letters to those states as well; there was even stamps: "The House of Correspondence of Pharaoh, life! Prosperity! health!"

It was during this excavation where Petrie discovered a secondary batch of *Amarna Letters* bearing the name of Akhenaten. During his time at Amarna, Petrie would discover faint structure remains of palaces, sun temples, domestic villas, and a dumping site-where there were remains of broken pottery, sculptures, and even glass-that made the experience worth it for Petrie. However, Petrie's greatest moment at Amarna was about to open the flood gates how Egyptologists- and the world- would view Akhenaten.

## A Stunning Revelation

When it was safe to go in, Petrie entered the remains of a large palace later dubbed **The Great Palace**. It was in the Great Palace where Petrie discovered three beautiful pavement

**The solar disc watching over Akhenaten's sarcophagus**

**William Flinders Petrie** *'Father of Pots'*

paintings in perfect preservation. These paintings were in two giant rooms known as the *Main Hall* and the *North Harem*. But the best prize of the Great Palace was in Room E of the North Hall called the *Great Pavement*- a 210 square meter painting depicting marsh life captured in a moment in time.

While the *Great Pavement* was a sight to behold, it was very fragile. As soon as he cleaned the paintings, Petrie coated the paintings in tapioca water- to keep the paintings fully stabled- and had a special shed placed over it, but his hopes to preserve the paintings were all in vain.

A local farmer, having been fed up with his fields being ruined by tourists- who consequently had to walk over his field to see the paintings up close-decided to hack up the *Great Pavement*. Fortunately for Petrie, he was able to salvage the broken pieces and can still be seen today at the Cairo Museum, yet they are a sad reminder of a great artistic treasure lost to vandalism

Despite his failure to protect the *Great Pavement* from destruction, Petrie discovered what appeared to be another dumping ground filled with broken pieces- and seals- of oil and wine jugs. From there, Petrie painstakingly glued back together the broken pieces and discovered Akhenaten had ruled as pharaoh for only seventeen years; and not twelve years as Lepsius had previously proposed. Though another important discovery, Petrie's next discovery would become one of the most iconic pieces of art in Egypt. Nearby the Great Palace, was another structure called the **King's House.**

As Petrie was walking in the dank and arid hallway, he came across an exquisite wall painting of Akhenaten tenderly playing with a child. Across from him was a woman- presumed to be

THE DECORATED PAVEMENT OF THE PALACE OF KHUNIATONU AT EL-AMARNA
Drawn by Faucher-Gudin, from lithographs by Flinders Petrie.

**Remnants of the Great Pavement**

**Akhenaten and his Queen tenderly playing and laughing with their three daughters (18th Dynasty)**

his wife- who too was tenderly playing with two children in loving embrace. Petrie was stunned. Traditionally, Egyptian art was rigid and one dimensional, but Akhenaten's depiction was far different. Never, in the history of Egyptian art had a pharaoh and his queen be presented with their children as a loving and happy family. Never had a pharaoh, in the history of Egypt, had been depicted so relaxed, so calm, so human.

It was as if Petrie was looking into another world. As Petrie gander at the painting, he noticed Akhenaten's children's heads were unusually elongated, and had the same "softness" as their

Parents. What could this mean? Did they suffer some form of disease or was it a stylistic choice? While contemplating, Petrie noticed the titular sun-disc arms were outstretched blessing Akhenaten and the royal family with an Egyptian *ankh* (meaning life).

At the time, Lepsius could not find the name of this god but now with accurate translations and preserved artifacts, we now had a name for this solar deity: **the Aten**. Petrie's discoveries at Amarna proved Lepsius' theories as factual: there was a pharaoh not named Bec-en-Aten but Akhenaten- who was overthrew Egypt's political and religious valuesin favor of worshipping the solar Aten. Now it was up to Egyptologists, scholars, and historians to put the pieces of Akhenaten's life back together and hoped to find the answers they were looking for, but Akhenaten's life would prove to be more problematic than any other pharaoh in recorded history.

# 3

# Prince of The Sun

For a little over a century, there had been prevailing contentions against Akhenaten. There are those in the academic community who praise Akhenaten as a radical idealist who challenged the myths of his country and tried- through his own hubris- to streamline Egypt's chaotic lists of deities into worshipping one single god. When Petrie first discovered the wall painting of Akhenaten and the royal family in 1892, he was fascinated by Akhenaten and the cult of the Aten. "Akhenaten stands out as perhaps the most original think that ever lived in Egypt, and one of the greatest idealists in the world".

Another influential commentator **James Henry Breasted**- founding father of American Egyptology- comments how Akhenaten was "the world's first revolutionist" who challenged Egypt's traditional conventions and firmly established a universal god that everyone could get behind. Academics felt the only ones to view Akhenaten's ideals in a positive light. The reverend **James Baikie** commented how

**Akhenaten presenting offerings before the Aten, as the Aten blesses Akhenaten with an ankh (18th Dynasty)**

Akhenaten "seems to have been the world's first pacifist," while further elaborating how "Egypt duly produced her great man, a man who in some respects is the greatest she ever produced."

Despite those who praise Akhenaten's as a revolutionary, there were those who condemned his actions as an act of heresy. German excavator **Ludwig Borchardt** blasted Akhenaten's reign as a "violent, bad exaggeration of good, old religious ideas, which throttled the possibility of their further development". While another, a man named **Jaroslav Cerny**, judged Akhenaten as nothing more "to be a dreamer and fanatic:" in latent terms he saw Akhenaten as insane to the end. Whether he was praised or condemned, Akhenaten is still seen as a heretical pharaoh- whose ideals of worshipping the Aten radically shifted the destiny of Egypt into uncertainty. When it came time to piece together his history, it would prove to be more troublesome then rewarding for the archaeologists and Egyptologists.

## Puzzling Akhenaten's Life

When it came time to piece together Akhenaten's life, Egyptologists became stuck. Why were they stuck? It has to do with the evidence that is currently known about Akhenaten. For starters, the evidence we do have about Akhenaten comes in the following;

1.  The discovery of the Amarna Letters in 1887
2.  Petrie's thorough excavation of Amarna between the seasons of 1891-1892
3.  Remains of a wine jug seal outside the Great Palace confirming Akhenaten's reign lasting no more than seventeen years.
4.  The recording of the tombs at Amarna
5.  The first records discovered at Thebes of a temple dedicated to the Aten
6.  Akhenaten's first five years on the throne in 1925.
7.  Further excavations at Amarna in 1912.

Think of Akhenaten's life as a giant jigsaw puzzle: you start putting the puzzle together with the pieces you are given and hope to recreate the image you see on the box; only to stop

**Akhenaten offering a sacrificial duck to the Aten; as the Aten in return blesses Akhenaten with the ankh (18th Dynasty)**

halfway when you ran out of pieces. That's how Egyptologists and historians felt when combing through the evidence. We only know half the image of Akhenaten's life. What we are still missing today about Akhenaten's life can be surmised like this

1. How old was he when he became pharaoh? When he died?
2. What was Akhenaten's childhood like, his upbringing, education?
3. Where did he grow up? When did he become obsessed with the Aten?

Questions like these would plague historians, but to compound matters is when new pieces of Akhenaten are discovered. At first, any new piece that could fit into the jigsaw puzzle excited historians, scholars, and Egyptologists; however, their excitement would turn sour when the new piece is disproven. With little evidence to go by, scholars, historians, and Egyptologists had to come up with new speculations on how Akhenaten rose to power, how he overthrew Egyptian tradition with one decisive action, and how his devotion to the Aten lead to his eventual downfall of Egypt.

## Early Life

Although we don't know of Akhenaten's life before his ascension, we do know- thanks to Lepsius early work at Amarna- Akhenaten and Amenhotep IV were the same person. At some point Amenhotep IV changed his name to Akhenaten. Therefore, we must speculate the early beginnings of Amenhotep IV's life. The life of Amenhotep IV begins with his birth in 1373 BC to the enigmatic **Queen Tiye** (*'The Great Royal Wife'*) and to the radiant Pharaoh **Amenhotep III** (*'The Magnificen*t'*).

 As to where he was born is highly speculative, yet we do know Akhenaten grew up in the Royal Palace called *Malkata* (Western Thebes); however, Amenhotep IV's life could've ended before it even started. When it came time to give birth, Egyptian mothers faced two unlikely scenarios: the mother has a miscarriage and could die from complications or both the mother and child die together.

These scenarios would not doubt had placed tremendous stress on Amenhotep III. To ensure the safety of Tiye-at the moment of childbirth- Amenhotep III had a special room prepared where Tiye could safely give birth to Amenhotep IV. This room contained images of the protector god Bes, the frog-headed goddess Heket, and the hippopotamus goddess Taweret and together, they would protect Tiye during childbirth and ensure Amenhotep IV to be delivered safely. As soon as Tiye went into labor, she was whisked away into the room where she was forced to balance herself on two bricks- using both her hands and feet- and if the pain was too excruciating, was given beer to ease the pain.

During the lengthy birth, priests were summoned to cast incantations to ward off evil spirits from harming Tiye and Amenhotep IV. Even with the mystical, Egyptian doctors had to take precautions and using their keen knowledge were able to bring Amenhotep IV into the world. Once the ordeal was over, Tiye was forced into quarantine for fourteen days- to cleanse her body from toxins during birth.

The name Amenhotep IV was given holds great significance in Egyptian culture. Names in Egypt held meaning and power and Amenhotep IV's name links him to his father, his great-grandfather (Amenhotep II), and to king of the gods, **Amun-Ra** (*'The Hidden One'*); which secured the relationship between mortals and gods. To be named after the highest of all Egyptian gods meant Amun-Ra acknowledged the birth of Amenhotep IV as worthy in his eyes, but as we will see, Amenhotep IV would reject his birth name and Amun-Ra.

Modern recreation of an Egyptian birthing room. Notice how Bes surrounds the room as a protective shield for the mother and child.

## Family

Although he was the son of Amenhotep IV and Tiye, Amenhotep IV wasn't their only child. Growing up, Amenhotep IV had four sisters Amenhotep IV had four sisters named **Sitamun**, **Henuttaneb**, **Isis**, and **Nebetah** and a little brother named **Thutmose** (named after the god of knowledge Thoth); however, in a shocking twist, it was the reverse: Thutmose was the eldest and Amenhotep IV was the youngest.

 It was believed that Amenhotep IV was the eldest- due to being named after Amun-Ra and his father- son because the first born was given the royal title *'Crown Prince'* who, upon the death of the pharaoh, would succeed become the next pharaoh of Egypt. But upon further examination, it was revealed that Amenhotep IV was indeed the second son of Amenhotep III and Tiye; while his older brother Thtumose, was next in line to take over their father's duties as pharaoh.

## Education

As a prince of Egypt, Amenhotep IV received the same education princes in Egypt had for centuries. By the time Amenhotep IV reached four, he would be thrusted to the *Kap*- the Royal Nursery which heavily secured, private, and located at the far end of the royal palace- to begin his education. He would be looked after by his *royal tutors* who oversaw the completion of their education and served as father figures for Amenhotep I- when his father was out- yet the tutors were always under constant and tense supervision. If they had failed to properly educate the prince, they could lose their title and any respect they had with the pharaoh. Currently, there are no surviving texts of the Kap's royal curriculum, but it's speculated that it was a standard education. One of the first

**Outline structure remains of Malkata (view from the air) where Amenhotep IV was born and spend his early life.**

lessons Amenhotep IV had to learn was the art of *hieratic writing*-cursive script used for day-to-day business and administrative documents- and would practice his writing on either wooden boards or broken pieces of pottery known as ostrica. Ostrica allowed the tutors, using red paint, to easily point out mistakes for the students to erase with water and try again. To coincide writing, the royal tutors made Amenhotep IV to read classical literature.

It was essential for every prince to be able to read, write, and memorize the classics to become a wise pharaoh. Amenhotep IV had to read *The Eloquent Peasant* and *The Tale of the Shipwreck Sailor* and probably inspired him early on in his life.

**Colossal bust of Amenhotep III; father of Amenhotep IV (located today at the British Museum)**

**Statuette of Amenhotep IV's mother, the beautiful Queen Tiye.**

To go with the classics, the royal tutors gave Amenhotep IV 'The Maxims of Ptahotep' a series of wisdom texts that instilled the ideals of morality of court life. As to his physical education, Amenhotep IV received training from top generals of the army on how to hold and shoot and arrow- and as he got older, taught how to ride a chariot.

## Outsider?

There has been contention amongst academics and Egyptologists what was Amenhotep IV's life growing up. There is no question he received proper education, but many suggest Amenhotep IV was an outsider. For instance, despite being named after the highest god in Egypt, Amun, and his father, Amenhotep IV was the second son-which meant Thutmose got more of the attention from their father. Why is this important? Amenhotep III over-saw the grooming of Thutmose to be his worthy successor; by enlisting the finest tutors throughout the empire to instruct him on education, mathematics, economics, diplomacy, and religion- under the 'hem netjer' (priests).

This meant, Amenhotep IV had gone unnoticed by his father and felt like an outsider. For instance, Canadian Egyptologist and archaeologist, Donald Redford saw Amenhotep IV as a "man deemed ugly by the accepted standards of the day, secluded, in the palace in his minority, certainly close with mother, possibly ignored by his father, outshone by his brother and sisters, unsure of himself." Another astute intellectual, **Arthur Weigall** (Chief Inspector of Antiquities) came up with a possible scenario to fill this missing piece in Amenhotep IV's life:

'He seems to have been a quiet, studious boy, whose thoughts wandered in fair places, searching for that happiness which his physical condition had denied him. His nature was gentle; his heart overflowed with love. He delighted, it would seem, to walk in the gardens of the palace, to hear birds singing, to watch the fish in the lake, to smell the flowers, to follow butterflies, to warm his small bones in the sunshine.'

If this is to be taken as fact, then it would explain why Amenhotep IV/Akhenaten-later on in his reign- had a strong affinity to the natural world. With a father who ignores him in favor of his older sibling- and possibly daughters- Amenhotep IV may have felt lonely, angered, hurt, and alone.

To compensate for his loneliness Amenhotep IV may have found comfort reading the classics, poetry, and spending time in the royal gardens; soaking in the rays of the Aten as he observed life. As to why both Redford and Weigall described Amenhotep IV/Akhenaten as "ugly" could be to the numerous representations of the pharaoh as having "softness" and an elongated skull, but if there was one person Akhenaten had a close tight relationship was his mother.

Tiye would have understood how Amenhotep IV was treated unfairly by Amenhotep III and like any mother would do, made sure to make his life as happy as possible. It may have been this close time with his mother Amenhotep IV learned about the Aten; how the sun disc was their family's patron god, how he blessed the world with his life-giving touch.

Tiye, when she wasn't attending Amenhotep III on affairs, may have encouraged Amenhotep IV's passion for the arts- it can be speculated Amenhotep IV during these years developed his artistic and poetic visions- which would've made his life a little bit better. But not everything in his life was doom and gloom. In fact, Amenhotep IV had the privilege to be born in Egypt's Golden Age, when Egypt was at the zenith of economic and military power; whose own father overseeing the most peaceful time in Egyptian history, but would become a proprietor of Akhenaten's ascension.

# 4

# Amenhotep III: The Pharaoh of Peace

In the last chapter, we discussed how Amenhotep IV was ignored by his father, Amenhotep III, in favor of personally overseeing Thutmose's education; including the era to which the young prince was born into: Egypt's Golden Age. But what was this Golden Age? To answer that, we need to go back to the year 285 BC when recently crowned **Ptolemy II of Philadelphos**, wanting to learn more about his new adopted homeland, commissioned a man named **Mantheo of Sebenytos** to write him a King's List.

As High Priest of Ra, Mantheo had access to historical records dating back for thousands of years. To make it easier for Ptolemy II to digest, he condensed the King's List into **dynasties**- in which instead of being connected to the pharaoh by blood, those who had political connections to the pharaoh could become pharaoh- from Narmer to Alexander the Great.

Today, Mantheo's extensive work is still used today as the framework on which Egypt's extensive history was built on; by

**Limestone head sculpt of Ptolemy II Philadelphos.**

dividing all the thirty-one pharaohs into not only a larger list but different time periods- that reflected the culture, history, and moments in each period. Here's what the list looks like today:

| Dynasty | Period(s) | Range (BC) |
| --- | --- | --- |
| 1st-2nd | The Early Dynastic | 3150-2686 |
| 3rd-6th | The Old Kingdom | 2686-2181 |
| 7th-10th | First Int. Period | 2181-2040 |
| 11th-13th | The Middle Kingdom | 2040-1782 |

| | | |
|---|---|---|
| 14th-17th | Second Int. Period | 1782-1570 |
| 18th-20th | The New Kingdom | 1570-1070 |
| 21st-31st | Third Int. Period | 1069-525 |
| Later Period | | 525-332 |
| Ptolemaic Period | | 332-31 |

The time period we are focusing on is called the New Kingdom when the pharaohs of this period were pristine warrior pharaohs; such as **Ahmose I** (*'the liberator'*) who liberated Egypt from two centuries of Hyksos rule-during the Second Intermediate Period- and was founder of the New Kingdom.

His successor, **Thutmose I**, lead the first wave of military conquest of the Near East- where he decimated the growing Kingdom of Mitanni- and stretched Egypt's borders farther than any pharaoh before him. Ten came the controversial **Queen Hatshepsut** -daughter of Thutmose I, and wife of Thutmose II-who deemed herself to be the rightful pharaoh of Egypt, usurped power from her stepson and presided over a time of architectural ingenuities such as the obelisk and her famous piece of all the mortuary temple at Djser-Djeseru (*'Holiest of Holy'*).

 Hatshepsut went as far as expanding Egypt's touch not through war, but through trade- including the trading expedition to the fabled *Land of Punt*. But it was under **Thutmose III** ('the Napoleon of Egypt') who at the *Battle of Megiddo* (the Biblical Armageddon) and further military conquests, conquered the Near East and ushered in a new Golden Age for Egypt. With the gold pouring from Nubia, and yearly donations from the conquered, Egypt became the wealthiest nation in the ancient world.

## The Dreaming Pharaoh

When we look at the ancestry of Amenhotep IV, he comes from a long line of warrior pharaohs, but not every pharaoh were warrior pharaohs. Case in point, Amenhotep IV's grandfather **Thutmose IV**. Son of pharaoh **Amenhotep II** and Queen **Taa**, Thutmose IV was one of several brothers who had claim to the throne. Thutmose IV had to compete with his brothers, but in the eyes of his parents saw him nothing more than a "puppy" not properly trained. One day

Thutmose IV was off hunting near the Giza Plateau, where, after a long day, came across the *Great Sphinx*- by this time, the Sphinx was buried head to toe in sand with only his head exposed. Thutmose IV had heard stories of his grandfather, Amenhotep II, about a solar deity named *Horemakhe*t (*'Horus of the Horizon'*) was affiliated with their family and decided to take a nap underneath the Sphinx's head when he was visited by *Horemakhet*-disguised as the Sphinx-claiming if he moved the sands encasing his body, he promised he would make him pharaoh.

As soon as Thutmose IV awakened, he ordered the sands to be removed from the Sphinx, to have an enclosure built so no sand would ever touch the Sphinx again. Thutmose IV would commemorate his prophetic dream in a stele- placed between the paws of the Sphinx- known as the 'Dream Stele':

'One of these days it happened that prince Thutmosis

came traveling at the time of midday. He rested in the shadow of this great god [the Great Sphinx]. Sleep and was at its zenith. Then he found the majesty of the noble god speaking from his own mouth like a father speaks to his son, saying 'Look at me, observe me, my son Thutmosis. I am your father Harmachis-Khepri-Re-Atum. I shall give to you kingship upon the land before the living.

You shall wear its white crown and its red crown upon the throne of Geb, the heir. The Land in its length and breadth will be yours, and everything which the eye of the lord-of-all illuminates. Good provisions will be for you from within the Two Lands, and the great produce of every country, and a lifetime great in years. My face belongs to me. Behold, my condition is like one illness, all my limbs being ruined. The sand of the desert, upon which I used to be, face me aggressively; and it is in order to make you do what is in my heart that I have waited. For I know that you are me son and my protector...'

Thutmose IV would go as far as proclaiming *Horemakhet* would be his personal god and have depictions of himself in the guise of the half-mortal and half-god to show his loyalty to

**Modern recreation of Thutmose IV's 'Dream Stele'.
Located at the Rosicrucian Museum, San Jose, CA.**

the solar deity. He even went as far as abandoning the image of the warrior in favor of the divine.

Thutmose IV would spend the rest of his reign overseeing the empire by conducting numerous diplomacies with the Mitanni. For instance, instead of launching military campaigns against the Mitanni, Thutmose IV took one of their princesses as his wife. This was to be a sign of good friendship with the Mitanni and with this new alliance came peaceful trade between Egypt and the Near East. As large caravans of goods began trickling from across the eastern Mediterranean into Egypt- with Egypt greatly benefiting from the surge of incoming wealth.

To commemorate this new era of prosperity, Thutmose IV issued his own building projects across Egypt;
with each monument pushing obsession with solar imagery- hinting what's to come in royal ideology. In 1401 BC, Thutmose IV and one of his minor wives, **Mutemwiya**, would have one son together: Amenhotep III but would pass on to the next life in 1390 BC; leaving the keys to the empire to a then ten year old Amenhotep III.

## The Young Amenhotep III

Although Thutmose IV died in 1390 BC, Amenhotep III was just ten years old. As Egypt's new pharaoh, the young Amenhotep III inherited a politically and financially stabled country, but unlike his warrior predecessors, the young Amenhotep III poured his focus on pushing Egyptian architecture and art to new heights-continuing the art of diplomacy like his father before him. Despite his young age, Amenhotep III made it his mission to let Egypt and the world know about him. He did this by commissioning the manufacturing of what would be his trademark: *Commemorative Scarabs*.

Carved from turquoise stones in the guise of scarabs, contained inscriptions- on the scarab's underbelly- Amenhotep III's feats and daily news. Today, these scarabs are considered the very first newspapers in recorded history. Traditionally, the scarab beetle was used as a design for protective charms such as the *Heart Scarab*- where it was placed underneath the mummy's bandages to protect his heart as the spirit travels the

The '*Marriage Scarab*'

underworld. Later, the scarab transitioned into a metaphor for the sun- where they viewed scarabs laying their eggs in a ball of dung as they used their legs to roll the ball and was seen as the sun making its journey across the heavens.

In the first twelve years on the throne, Amenhotep III produced large quantities of *Commemorative Scarabs* where they would make their way across the country and eastern Mediterranean. The first scarab Amenhotep III issued was the Marriage

Scarab. Written in Year 2, it was the announcement of Amenhotep III's marriage to his great love Tiye:

> 'Living Horus, Strong bull appearing in Truth; he of the Two Ladies, establishing laws, pacifying the Two Lands; Golden Falcon Great of valour, who smites the Asiatics; King of Upper and Lower Egypt, Nebmaatre; son of Re, Amenophis-ruler of Thebes, who gives life; and the great royal wife Tiye, may she chariot [again]. The number of wild bulls he took hunting: 40 wild bulls total...She is the wife of the mighty king whose southern boundary is at Karoy, whose northern at Naharin.'

This was unusual for a pharaoh to announce his wedding to the public since royal weddings were usually done in private, yet Amenhotep III wanted everyone to know about their new Queen.

One of Amenhotep III's favorite pastimes was hunting wild game. The most common scarab to be produced and reproduced was the *Lion Heart Scarab* where it describes Amenhotep III hunting and killing over hundred lions by himself; however, Egyptologists see this as nothing more than propaganda to paint Amenhotep III as a great warrior who conquered the forces of chaos in Egypt.

## Queen Tiye

Unlike any queen before her, Tiye was seen by Amenhotep III not only as his partner in life and at court but was a great influencer at court- taking an active role as Amenhotep III's

**The 'Lion Scarab' underside (on top);
beetle motif (bottom)**

**Head sculpt of the young Amenhotep III. 18<sup>th</sup> Dynasty**

Tiye was unlike any queen in the history of Egypt: she was a commoner. Traditionally, the pharaoh would pick his queen within the royal family- to keep the royal bloodline within the family- but Amenhotep III was the first to break traditional convention by choosing Tiye as his queen. Even at twelve years old, the bond Amenhotep III and Tiye had was incredibly strong.

Despite Tiye not being a member of the royal family, she wasn't an average commoner. Her parents, Yuya and Tuya, were well established members of the elite. Yuya held the distinction of being a notable landowner bearing numerous titles such as '*Overseer of the King's Horses,*' '*his majesty's lieutenant,* '*commander of the chariotry,*' and *God's father*'; while Tuya was a participator in religious centers and was bestowed titles as '*Singer of Hathor,*' '*Singer of Amun,*' and '*King's Mother of the King's Great Wife.*'

Now as Egypt's new queen, Tiye was able to enjoy a life of luxury at Amenhotep III's court. She indulged herself in the new garments sweeping the nation and even wore them to court. With Amenhotep III's encouragement, Tiye participated at court and go over state affairs. She was even allowed to write and send her own letters to foreign kings- who wrote back to Tiye as she was Amenhotep III himself.

These letters presented Tiye as a wise and respected queen amongst other rulers. As an equal to her husband, Tiye began being depicted alongside Amenhotep III's divine kingship. If Amenhotep III was Amun-Ra, then Tiye was Amun-Ra's wife Mut. From there, she began incorporating the goddess Hathor's cow horns and solar disc. Tiye went as far as having herself being associated with the vulture goddess *Nekhbet*- who guided the sun across the heavens- and served as a symbol of support to Amenhotep III's mortal reign.

Although she was infused with divine iconography within her statues and wardrobe, Tiye was given another, if not, fearsome role. Egyptian artists had Tiye being depicted as the sphinx as she stomps over the pharaoh's enemies. This was a first for any Egyptian queen. From the beginning of his coronation, Tiye would stand by her husband's side. She would be depicted standing alongside Amenhotep III as true equals in power and stature, accompanying him to *Royal Jubilees* (festivals); while

**The Guorb Head of Queen Tiye-made from yew and acacia wood- as she wears the horns of Hathor. 18<sup>th</sup> dynasty**

**Fragment Letter written by Queen Tiye**

while her name would be placed on minor objects such as jewelry, pottery, and faience- kohl like confetti used to shower audiences at jubilees.

One of the best pieces to come from this time was the *Gurob Head of Queen Tiye'* in which the sculptor, **Iuty**- personally chosen by Tiye herself- carved Tiye's image with accurate wrinkles around the mouth, and heavier eye lids, Hathor's horns, the twin plumes of shu, and the solar disc. Despite not being renowned today like Hatshepsut, Tiye's role as queen shook the status quo by being gifted with powers equal to the pharaoh; all the while not having to usurp power away for political gain. Her time on the throne would have a deep impact on how Amenhotep IV/Akhenaten treated and presented his own queen.

## Diplomatic Genius

To keep peace throughout the empire, Amenhotep III would rule his kingdom not through military campaigns like his forefathers, but with words. Amenhotep III decided he would use Egypt's overabundance of wealth to exploit his enemies into forgoing their possessions in exchange for Egypt's continual protection. Amenhotep III began implementing his father's practice by marrying foreign princesses. The practice of marrying foreign princesses was common in the ancient world when dealing with diplomatic negotiations.

After marrying these princesses, they would join other princesses throughout the empire in the royal harem. The royal harem was usually connected to the pharaoh's royal palace and was off-limits to the elite except for the pharaoh. It was the duty of the pharaoh to prove he was fertile and any male child he had with his minor wives or those in the harem had a chance of becoming the pharaoh's favorite.

 Amenhotep III's harem had the distinguished reputation of containing the most beautiful daughters from Syria, to as far as Babylonia (modern Iraq). For the Egyptians, it was an act of diplomacy which sealed the relationship between the Pharaoh and the foreign ruler as *"Brothers."* We see this brotherly exchange between Amenhotep III and the king of Babylonia:

'Say to Nimmuarea [Amenophis III], the king of Egypt, my

brother: thus Burra-Buriyash, the king of Karduniash [Babylonia], your brother. For me all goes well. For you, your household, your wives, your sons, your country, your magnates, your hopes, your chariots may all go well. Just as previously you and my father were friendly to one another, you and I should be friendly to one another. Between us, anything else whatsoever is not even to be mentioned.

Write to me for what you want from my country so that it may be taken to you, and I will write to you for what I want from your country so that it may be taken to me…'

In exchange for marrying one of their princesses, Amenhotep III would give his brothers the one thing they desperately wanted from Egypt: gold. In another *Amarna Letter*, we can get an idea of Amenhotep III's brothers' plea for Egypt's overabundance of gold:

'As to the gold I wrote [to pharaoh] about: send me whatever is on hand as much as possible…so I can finish the work I am engaged on… I will give you my daughter. So please send me the gold…

Gold was the number one currency used in diplomatic exchange and since Egypt had a continuous flow of gold flowing from Nubia's gold mines, Amenhotep III had leverage over his brothers. However, Egypt almost lost their precious gold. In Year 13 of Amenhotep III's reign, an insurrection occurred in Nubia and if they succeed, Egypt would've lost their precious commodity. Without mercy, the insurrection was put down. If Egypt were to lose their gold, they were nothing, worthless.

Everyone of Amenhotep III's brothers wanted a piece of Egypt's gold. As **Tushratta**, king of Mitanni, once wrote: '*In Egypt, gold is more plentiful than dirt.*' These rulers would always beg for Egypt's gold and Amenhotep III, in kind, would honor their requests by giving them their precious gold, however, Amenhotep III would only give enough gold to satisfy them until they came crawling back begging for more.

 This is what made Amenhotep III a genius. Since Amenhotep III had the gold and the power, he had absolute power to take away his brother's gold privileges whenever he felt like it. If his brothers gave him their respect and loyalty, then he would honor his word by giving them gold to fill their own royal treasury.  In a larger cache of the Amarna Letters, records Amenhotep III's diplomatic relationship with lesser rulers in Syria and Palestine.

When one of the rulers called Amenhotep III "brother," Amenhotep III had to remind these lesser nations were expected to pay him their annual tribute- to gain the pharaoh's loyalty and respect and nothing more. In fact, these lesser nations were so afraid of Amenhotep III's punishment, they began referring to the pharaoh as their own king! We see this unequal practice between Amenhotep III and a Levantine ruler:

'To the king, my lord, my god, my sun, the sun from the sky.
This is a message from Shur-Ashar, the ruler of Akhtishana,
who is your servant, the dirt at your feet, the groom of your
horse. I prostate myself at the feet of the king, my lord, my
god, my sun, the sun from the sky, seven times on the
stomach and on the back. I have listened carefully to the
order of the commissioner of my king, my lord very
carefully. Who is the dog that would not obey the orders of
the king, his lord the sun from the sky, the son of the sun.'

Even though Amenhotep III married princesses from his
brothers, there came a time when Amenhotep III had to draw
the line. When one brother was eager to marry an Egyptian
princess, Amenhotep III angrily rejected his brother's plea:
"From time immemorial no daughter of the king of Egypt is
given to anyone."

Amenhotep III knew if he were to marry one of his princesses
to one of his brothers, their children (male) would have a claim
to the Egyptian throne. He didn't want to see Egypt undergo
foreign subjugation as his forefathers went through under the
Hyksos, but even if Amenhotep III went through with this
blasphemy, it would've backfired. Internally, the Egyptian
people would see it as the pharaoh going against Maat and
allowing chaos to rule Egypt again.

On the international scale, this act seen by other nations as an
act of favoritism which could lead to political instability and
even war. Amenhotep III decided the best outcome was to
reject any further pleas for an Egyptian princess from his
brothers. The only thing his brothers could do was to accept

and continue this unequal relationship in fear of losing their privileges to Egypt's gold.

## Grand Architect

From the moment he came to existence, Amenhotep III inherited the title "ruler of Thebes," and with the absence of war, Amenhotep III had a lot of free time on his hands. He had all the gold in the world but didn't know what to spend it on. It wasn't until he looked at Thebes outdated foundations that gave him an idea: he would spend Egypt's wealth on rebuilding Thebes into a cosmopolitan city. would be regarded as one of Egypt's greatest builders (and visionary) since the time of the Great Pyramids. At the beginning of his reign, Amenhotep III had ordered the reopening of stone quarries and to conscript workers to get to work.

Throughout his reign, Amenhotep III's architectural feat was felt across the empire; from Nubia to Saqqara- where he had the first chapel dedicated to the sacred Apis Bull (the earthly incarnation of Memphis' patron god, Ptah- there was no place Amenhotep III left his mark. At the island of Abu, Amenhotep III had commissioned a new shrine for the ram-headed creator god, Khnum; however, his greatest architectural feats were in Thebes.

At Thebes, Amenhotep III ordered his chief architect, **Amenhotep**, **Son of Hapu**, to oversee the construction of his most famous monuments known as the '*Colossi of Memnon*'- named after the Greek hero *Memnon*. These colossi were two herculean seated statues of Amenhotep III- carved entirely from two seven-hundred-pound pink quartzite- who stood before his **Mortuary Temple**. During the Nile's **Akhet**

**season**- from July to October was the annual flood- the statues would be submerged in the Nile for a period of several months until they re-emerged; this acted as a symbol of rebirth, rejuvenating Amenhotep III's mortuary temple for eons.

These statues gained notoriety when, in 27 BC, an earthquake damaged the northern statue- causing the statue to unleash and unworldly moan. However, this moan was due to heat from the sun building pressure within the statue's cracks and as is it released the pressure, gave the signature moan. For a time, it became a tourist destination in the ancient world until the statue went under repairs in the Third Century AD by Roman emperor Septimius Severus; did the moans cease.

The '*mansion of millions of years*' itself was an architectural feat of ingenuity in Egypt. Located on the western bank of the Nile, Amenhotep III's mortuary temple was an unprecedented ninety miles with the complex beams coated in twenty-six-foot-tall colossi statues of Amenhotep III as the god of the underworld, Osiris. At one end of the temple contained a herculean seated statue of Amenhotep III and Tiye- standing around twenty-three feet tall- while at the northern entry way was covered with granite statues of Amenhotep III. In total, the temple was comprised of three gigantic courts with each court having their own gateway guarded by Amenhotep III himself.

 While many of the deity's statues in the temple were carved from a black stone, known as granodiorite, Amenhotep III's was carved from either red or golden quartzite. The color black was the symbol of rebirth while the colors red and gold meant Amenhotep III's close connection to the sun- when the Nile flooded, it symbolized not only Amenhotep III's control over

**Structural outline of Amenhotep III's Mortuary Temple (top)**

**Sketch of the 'Colossi of Memnon' (bottom)**

**Modern Day 'Colossi of Memnon,' 18th dynasty, Thebes**

death but life as well. Once his Mortuary Temple was constructed, Amenhotep III set his eyes on **Ipetsut** (The Temple of Karnak).

He ordered a new entrance to be constructed for the temple complex, with an additional gateway to be installed at the temple's southern end that led to the temple of the goddess **Mut**. From there, Amenhotep III adorned the temple with the finest stone sculptures of the lion-headed goddess Sekhmet-

whose association with the sun god Ra as the god's "eye of Ra". Further north, Amenhotep III had new temples made for the goddess of truth Maat and Montu- the son of Amun-Ra and Mut. Despite his large architectural feats, and goodwill to his brothers, it seemed the empire would continue to shine brightly; however, the sun always casts a shadow and there was

one particular shadow lurking in the background that has been around since the formation of the New Kingdom, and it was getting bigger.

# 5

# Corruption, the Aten, and The Dazzling Orb

At the time of Amenhotep III's ascension, Egypt was keeping a dark secret if exposed, would've had disastrous consequences: priestly corruption. From the very beginning of the New Kingdom, the pharaoh and High priest's relationship were inextricably linked together. For starters, Hatshepsut used religious propaganda to claim Amun-Ra was her father and as his daughter, had full autonomy of the throne of Egypt. This corrupt support from the high priest and Amun-Ra priesthood indirectly gifted them with political power in the process.

Then there was Thutmose III who donated large portions of his spoils of war and gold to the Temple of Karnak- unknowingly filling the pockets of the priests. It was the duty of the **High Priest** to not only promote, reinforce, and idolize the pharaoh but was the keeper of Egypt's wealth. However, this once close relationship began to fall apart. Throughout the New Kingdom, the Temple of Karnak had used their considerable amount of wealth to buy land; with each passing year, the high priest securing more and more land for Amun-Ra. So much, the high

**Black granite statue of a High Priest of Egypt, wearing linen clothing and sporting a leopard skin over his left shoulder.**

the high priest inadvertently created a mini kingdom within Egypt; by the end, they owned one third of the land in Egypt and territories in the Near East; in this one third, the priests owned many orchids, farms, granaries akin to the pharaoh.

The priests even went as far as transferring their position of power to their son as if they were the pharaoh. With one third of Egypt's land under their belt, they needed a workforce to till the land and as a result, owned large hordes of slaves working and serving the priests. Due to the increasing influx of economic and political power, the priests (and Amun) became just as powerful if not more than the pharaoh himself. What was more dangerous than economic and political power?

Having spiritual power over the pharaoh and the people. All the high priests had to do was make a request to the pharaoh to donate more gold due to the temple to secure Amun's continual protection and blessing, while guilting the pharaoh into thinking what's best for the people. These priests were abusing their power and trust to not only the people but the pharaoh; through deception and greed to accumulate power. At any moment, the high priest could seize power for himself with a simple snap of his finger, but simply does not. Why was this?

The answer is simple: they had leverage over the people, the wealth, and even the pharaoh-who by this point would've acted more as a puppet ruler to the priests who had power- that was more than enough for them. If the high priest saw Amenhotep III going against the "will" of Egypt, he could use this as an instigator to fund an open armed revolt against the pharaoh and overthrow him; however, the priesthood had underestimated Amenhotep III and things were about to change.

## Rise of the Aten

Although Amenhotep III began worshipping the Aten throughout his reign, why did he continue to worship Amun-Ra? At Luxor, Amenhotep III had his workers rebuild Amun-Ra's "southern palace" and on the temple's western wall depicts his mother Mutemwiya and his father Thutmose IV or rather Amun in the guise as his father; with the texts describing Amenhotep III's conception:

**Wall relief of Amenhotep III and Mutemwia. 18<sup>th</sup> dynasty, Located at the Temple of Luxor**

'Amenhotep-ruler-of-Thebes is the name of the child that I have placed in your womb…. He shall exercise potent kingship in this entire land…He shall rule the Two Lands of Ra forever.'

Like Hatshepsut before him, this was again to show how Amun-Ra was responsible for the divine birth of the pharaoh and the legitimization of the dynasty in Amun-Ra's eyes. So, when does Amenhotep III discover the corruption? The problem is, we simply do not know.

If Amenhotep III had discovered corruption amongst the priestly class, then he would have exploited it, only he didn't. There is no text, but it can be speculated that if he did exploit this corruption, there could've been major backlash. The Egyptian people hated change and if Amenhotep III implemented the closure of Amun-Ra's temple's, the people would be angry; or the high priest could turn the pharaoh against the people and lead a coups d'état to overthrow him without lifting a finger.

However, it is speculated that Amenhotep III saw the priests getting more powerful and probably felt threatened by them. If Amenhotep III was going to exploit the corruption of the priesthood, he had to be smart, not rush in his decision, and come up with a perfect counter to quell the continued power of the priestly class. Amenhotep III was in a pickle: if he stuck to the status quo, he would be enabling the priests- albeit high priest- to continue to grow more in power and stature with little to no resistance. Or Amenhotep III could go all in on exploiting the corruption and face backlash, yet there was a third option

Amenhotep III hadn't considered. What if he diverted power away from Amun-Ra and give it to a new god? If his fore-fathers had promoted Amun-Ra as their personal god-during the early days of the Middle Kingdom and the Second Intermediate Period- then Amenhotep III would promote the ever-growing popular Aten as his personal god. During the construction at Luxor, Amenhotep III insisted the renovated temple complex be an open court. Why is this important? This was the beginning of Amenhotep III's growing affiliation with solar worship.

Traditionally, temples in Egypt were enclosed, dark, and closed off, but open courts were unroofed, and opened for sun worship. Once completed, Amenhotep III personally instructed his loyal architects to construct any and every temple in Egypt or abroad to be constructed as an open court and have connections with solar worship. Where did the Aten come from and why did it catch the eye of Amenhotep III?

## The Aten's Origins

Solar worship was no stranger to Egyptian civilization; in fact, we can trace solar worship back to the very beginning of Egyptian civilization. To the Egyptians, they viewed the sun as an omnipresent god who revealed himself to his people and was always present. They began referring to the sun as Ra or Re. In the last chapter, we discussed the scarab beetles was viewed as a solar deity when it rolled the ball dung- seen as the sun moving across the heavens- and the larvae hatching from within was new life. They called this deity **Khepri** *('coming into being')*.

The final form of the sun was in the form of **Re-Horakhty** (*'Re [is] Horus of the Horizon'*) and was the amalgamation of the falcon headed Horus and Ra; with Re-Horakhity seen as the sun rising from the darkness. Aten was originally Re-Horakhty's visible body but by the time of Amenhotep II, the Aten became the titular solar disc or orb- with the additions of the sun's rays becoming outstretched hands holding the ankh. The Aten was even referenced in the classical tale, *The Tale of*

*Sinuhe* (written around 1900 BC). During the Eighteenth Dynasty, there was a massive influx of foreigners and merchants wanting to settle in the Delta. As a result, these foreigners would intermarry their cultures with Egypt's and helped transform Egypt into one of the world's first cosmopolitan nation in the ancient world.

Due to the mingling of two cultures came the resurgence of solar worship. Under the reign of Thutmose IV, the Aten began growing in popularity with the public. Thutmose IV, observing this new phenomenon began identifying himself as the Aten itself. A prime of example of the Aten's new popularity can be seen on the *Aten Scarab* where it describes the first early reference to the Aten under Thutmose IV:

> 'The prince of Naharin [Mitanni], bearing their gift, behold Menkheprure [Thutmosis IV] as he comes forth from his palace. They hear his voice like that of a son of Nut, his bow in his hand like the son of the successor of Shu. If he arouses himself to fight, with the Aten before him, he destroys the mountain countries, trampling the desert countries, treading as far as Naharin and Karoy, in order to make the inhabitants of foreign lands like the subjects of the rule of the Aten forever.'

While the inscription of the *Aten Scarab* commemorates Thutmose IV's military campaign in the North, it's the mention of the Aten that interests us. This was the first time the Aten was used not only in Egypt but on an international scale. For

**Relief fragment of the Aten as it outstretches its life-giving rays.
Rosicrucian Museum, San Jose, Ca**

**Amenhotep III presented as Horemakhet (the Sphinx) as he presents offerings to the sun. 18<sup>th</sup> dynasty**

Amenhotep III, he was not just an Egyptian pharaoh but an international one and what better way to appeal both groups.

## *'The Dazzling Orb'*

Amenhotep III knew to win both groups was to be in favor of the Aten. He did this first at the *Temple at Sumenu* where he merged the crocodilian god Sobek with Ra to create they hybrid Sobek-Ra. He took great pains to make himself associated with the solar deities as "Ra's chosen one" and "heir of Ra", and desired to embody their solar power; however, during his first royal jubilee in 1361, Amenhotep III shook the status quo by proclaiming himself as a creator god.

In the past, pharaohs had proclaimed their own divinities- while boasting their godlike powers through reliefs- but Amenhotep III was the first to outright claim he was a literal god. He even went as far as depicting himself in a new style: enlarged almond-shaped eyes, fuller lips, and high cheekbones, but Amenhotep III took it one step further by proclaiming to be the *'Dazzling Orb of all Lands'* or *'dazzling Aten.'* At the *Temple of Soleb* for instance in accordance with his dedication to solar worship- Amenhotep III had his architects enlarge the temple's small shrine into two large solar open courts. Here, Amenhotep III had gigantic statues of himself created with depictions of himself making offerings to himself as the 'Dazzling Orb.'

At Thebes, Amenhotep III ordered his architects to build a new ceremonial city for the festivities. Personally, choosing the site on the Delta's western bank, Amenhotep III issued the construction of his *Malkata* palace- *'Palace of the Dazzling Orb* and the *House of the Rejoicing"*. Nearly a mile in length,

**Ruins of the Temple of Soleb (located in modern Ethiopia). 18th Dynasty**

**Faience kohl tube bearing the cartouches of Amenhotep III and Tiye. 18<sup>th</sup> Dynasty**

**Seated statue of Amenhotep III. 18<sup>th</sup> Dynasty**

*Malkata* came with its own villas, an administrative district, and a secondary palace where the royal family lived. Coated on the ceilings were imported paintings from the Minoan civilization; with every room contained elegant multicolored glasses, perfume, and ointment jars- glass making became one of Amenhotep III's favorites. In Year 11, Amenhotep III ordered an artificial harbor to be constructed at *Malkata's* western and eastern sectors as gift for his beloved Tiye; with each harbor measuring at half a mile long. The western harbor- referred to as *Birket Habu*- served as a pathway for Amenhotep III's royal barge during his jubilees.

Today, the western harbor remains as a dumping ground and the only way to see its size is by air; while the eastern harbor has disappeared altogether, but in the time of Amenhotep III, these harbors acted as the heavens. Amenhotep III- in the guise of the *'Dazzling Orb'*-traveled across the water on the royal barge. This was Amenhotep III recreating the sun's journey- traveling across the sky- as he and Tiye, covered in golden garments, travel across the lake to the royal festivities.

Upon his departure, Amenhotep III had his royal courtiers, officials, acquaintances, and acolytes, join him in a special ceremony. In this ceremony, Amenhotep III blessed them with gifts of golden ornaments- in the form of fish and ducks- and golden necklaces. These gifts were seen as Amenhotep III- as the *'Dazzling Aten'*- blessing those close to him with the gift of life; as the Aten blesses the world with its life-giving rays. From there, a great banquet was held between Amenhotep III, Tiye, and their loyal followers. As they reached the eastern harbor, the loyal members gazed at Amenhotep III and Tiye covered in head to toe in gold as a unified Aten.

Once boarded, the courtiers took up the oars and helped row the royal barge across the lake to the western harbor; where Amenhotep III stepped off and put on a new set of golden garments representing the sun's descent into the underworld at night- as the courtiers once more rowed the royal barge and recreating the journey through the underworld. Over the next two jubilees, Amenhotep III would recreate the same ceremonies all over again. It appears Amenhotep III was beginning to win the people over with the Aten, but things were about to take a drastic turn.

# 6

# Amenhotep IV: The Accidental Pharaoh

Throughout his reign, Amenhotep III had been grooming Thutmose into becoming a worthy successor. When Thutmose was approaching adulthood, Amenhotep III awarded his son a position as the new *High Priest of Ptah*; a tradition for every crown prince must undertake before taking the throne. As the new high priest, Thutmose was responsible for guarding the temple's most sacred animal: Apis bull. To the Egyptians, every animal was considered an embodiment of the gods-while acting as an anchor to the mortal world.

The Apis was the living image of the craftsmen god *Ptah*; who traditionally was depicted as a mummified man with blue skin, while holding the was-djed-ankh scepter. As the new high priest, Thutmose would be the intermediary between the mortal world and to Ptah. It seemed everything was going fantastic for Amenhotep III, unfortunately for the pharaoh (and the dynasty) things were about to be turned upside down.

In 1361 BC, Thutmose, heir apparent to Amenhotep III, unexpectedly vanishes from history. To this day, it's still unclear if Thutmose disappeared, was murdered, or personally erased by Amenhotep IV to get revenge towards his old brother getting all the attention from their father. Or the most recurring theory that Thutmose was the biblical **Moses**- which means the **Book of Exodus** (second book in the Bible) took place around this time, but it has been disproven. For now, though, we just don't know what happened to Thutmose. What is currently accepted that Thutmose was in his mid-twenties when he disappeared.

The only surviving text of Thutmose's existence comes from a tiny sarcophagus for his pet cat with the inscription *"the Osiris, the lady cat'*. Amenhotep III was now in trouble. He had spent two decades getting his oldest son ready to take on the responsibilities of the throne, and with his health beginning to decline he would be dooming Egypt without a suitable heir. In Amenhotep III's eyes, the disappearance/death of Thutmose was now a complete waste of time and money, but luckily for him, he still had Amenhotep IV. Whether it was karma or fate, Amenhotep IV was thrusted into the limelight for the first time as Amenhotep III declared him to be his heir.

## Co-Regency

There has been contention to how long Amenhotep IV co-ruled with his father. Traditionally, co-regency only happened when two kings ruled at the same time. This went against Egypt's tradition of kingship- which stated only one pharaoh could rule at a time- however, Amenhotep III was desperate. By this time

**Head sculpt of Amenhotep IV (18<sup>th</sup> Dynasty)**

in his life, Amenhotep III was in terrible shape with depictions showing the once youthful *Dazzling Orb* to be morbidly obese, wore loose fitting robes as his back issues caused him to slump. He was running out of time. Having his second son succeed him proved to be more problematic than a solution.

Although his dynasty would live on through his son, Amenhotep IV wasn't properly trained to take on this kind of responsibility. Therefore, Amenhotep IV had to learn about his future duties alongside his father. Amenhotep III forced the young Amenhotep IV to study government, economics, religion, and so on. When he wasn't in court, Amenhotep IV was forced to attend with his father on temple visits for communal prayer and offerings. As to how old Amenhotep IV when he co-ruled with his father is debatable. Since he was now co-regent, Amenhotep III may have awarded Amenhotep IV the title of *High Priest of Ptah*, but's unknown if this happened or not.

For instance, scholars argued that Amenhotep IV was thirteen years old when he began his co-rulership and after the death of Amenhotep III, he would have been eighteen years old; that meant the co-regency lasted for only five years. Many scholars who argued Amenhotep IV's co-regency lasted more than a decade and didn't become pharaoh until he was in his mid-twenties. But it may have been during this time both father and son connected over their obsession of the Aten.

After all, Amenhotep IV had grown up being dazzled by the solar imagery of Ra, and the imageries of the Aten at the jubilees and the teachings by Tiye. Amenhotep III may have informed Amenhotep IV about the lingering corruption, but this is very speculative at best. In either 1353 or 1351 BC, Amenhotep III, the pharaoh who ruled with his words and not by the sword, dies; leaving the empire and his legacy to a now adult Amenhotep IV.

## The Ascension of Amenhotep IV

It's unclear where Amenhotep IV was crowned, but it's likely he was crowned at Thebes in 1353/1351 BC. Now as the tenth pharaoh of the Eighteenth Dynasty, Amenhotep IV could now implement his master plan: to permanently distance himself with Amun-Ra and the gods and focus his devotion on the Aten

**Standing statue of Amenhotep IV (18<sup>th</sup> Dynasty)**

but didn't. What could be the reason he failed to implement his plan early? Could it be he wasn't confident in his plan working? Or, due to his weak training he needed more time to understand the duties of the pharaoh?

It's more likely Amenhotep IV didn't properly plan how he would implement his religious policies-and the very possible backlash from the people. So, in the first two years of his reign, Amenhotep IV had to secretly map out his plan in secret. In the meantime, he would put on a "face" to the public. In his first year on the throne, Amenhotep IV continued to worship the gods, and being a good son, fulfilled his father's last projects by completing and decorating the entrance way at Ipetsut.

From there, Amenhotep IV added his own reliefs as a warrior pharaoh smiting his enemies; ordering his architects to construct a new temple for Amun at Nubia. It appeared Egypt was in good hands with their new pharaoh. Even the king of Tyre was in awe of Amenhotep IV. 'I fall at the feet of the king, my lord, seven and seven times. I am the dirt beneath the sandals of the king, my lord. My lord is the sun who comes forth over all lands day by day.'

Although Amenhotep IV was pharaoh, he was referred to as the "sun" like his father before him, but this unequal relationship between Egypt and its brothers was still an ongoing issue- the least of Amenhotep IV concerns. After two years of thorough planning, it was time for Amenhotep IV to enact the first part of his plan.

## Amenhotep IV Shows His True Colors

The first year of Amenhotep IV's reign went soothingly well for Egypt. Their new pharaoh was continuing the policies of their predecessor, gold was continuing to pour in from Nubia's gold mines, morale was high, and relations with Egypt's brothers were on good terms. For instance, when Amenhotep III died, Tushratta wrote the widowed Tiye lamenting the loss of his brother:

> 'When my brother Nimmureya [Amenhotep III] went to his fate it was reported. When I heard what was reported, nothing was allowed to be cooked in a pot. On that day I wept, on that day I took neither food or water.'

**Side view of Amenhotep IV head sculpt (18<sup>th</sup> Dynasty)**

All rulers across the eastern Mediterranean hoped to maintain the same level of good relations with *Napkureya-* pharaohs were given an extra name to coincide their own name- with Tushratta hoping to continue their relationship:

> 'But when they said Napureya (Amenophis IV), the eldest son of Nimmureya and Tiye, his principal wife, is exercising the kingship in his place, then I spoke as follows 'Napkureya, his eldest son, now exercises the kingship in his place. Nothing whatsoever is going to be changed from the way it was before.'

At first glance, it appeared Amenhotep IV was going to continue this practice with his fellow brothers, that is until the angry letters pouring in. King Tushratta started writing angry letters to the court of Amenhotep IV, demanding why the young pharaoh was withholding his end of the bargains.

> 'My brother has not sent the gold statues that your father was going to send. You have sent plated ones of wood. Nor have you send me goods that your father was going to send me, but reduces them secretly.'

If this wasn't a warning sign that Amenhotep IV didn't care about the needs of his brothers, then it was about to get more heated. Another ruler by the name of **Suppilulimas**, King of the Hittites, angrily wrote to Amenhotep IV over the young pharaoh's lack of respect between kings.

'And now, as to the tablet you sent me, why did you put your name over my name? And who now is the one who upsets the good relations between us, and is such conduct the accepted practice? My brother, did you write to me with peace in mind…?'

We can see the early signs of Akhenaten within these letters- in which Amenhotep IV is presenting himself as an omnipresent god- however, in the eyes of his brothers, they deemed Amenhotep IV's actions as acting like a spoiled child and needed to start acting more like an adult. 'You're no linger a child, but a man; behave like one."

Could this be Amenhotep IV getting back at his father for years of neglect in favor of his relationship with Thutmose and his brothers? It's tough to say since there is no written record of Amenhotep IV's response to this problem, but it's more likely Amenhotep IV was trying to go against the status quo and felt the gold belonged to him and not his brothers.

## *Gempaaten*

In Year 2, Amenhotep IV enacted part two of his plan by issuing his own building project. At the quarry site of **Gebel Silsila**, there is a stele carved onto the walls of the quarry to commemorate this moment:

'The first occasion that his Person [Amenophis IV] laid a charge on the king's scribe, the general Amun…to carry out all the works projects…and on the leaders of the army to perform a great forced-labor-duty of quarrying sandstone, in order to fashion the great benben of Horakhti, Light which is in Aten.'

Once securing conscripted workers, Amenhotep IV sent his workers to Memphis and Heliopolis to begin the construction of solar temples. These temples would be dedicated not to Amun but for the Aten. After completing their task, Amenhotep IV ordered them to go to the eastern edge of Ipetsut and immediately work on his masterpiece.

Amenhotep IV, after studying from his father's own projects, deliberately chose to construct his new temple on the eastern edge. Why on the east? For starters, the new temple was beyond the confines of Amun's domain with its position on the eastern bank pointing towards the Aten's sunrise. On this deserted mudflat, Amenhotep IV's grand temple was realized and named it **Gempaaten** ('*the Aten is found*').

In its heyday, *Gempaaten* was a gigantic open court temple with its pillars covered by twenty-five-foot statues of Amenhotep IV- all carved from a single block of limestone- sporting the double crown of Egypt or the nemes headdress. The crown's feathers- of the god Shu- subtly hinted Amenhotep IV's proclamation that he was the god Shu, and the Aten was his father (Ra), but when the people took a gander at their pharaoh for the first time, they were horrified beyond relief.

## Amenhotep IV's New Look

From the beginning of his reign, it was always in the back of Amenhotep IV's mind to present himself different from his father and predecessors. Traditionally, the pharaoh was mandated to be presented as a youthful and superhuman to the world; however, Amenhotep IV decided to break from traditional convention and present himself as the real thing and not manufactured. But what did these depictions look like?

Although these depictions are viewed today as otherworldly, they may have been the genuine look of Amenhotep IV: his face was long, slender with a droopy chin, with almond-shaped eyes, exaggeratedly elongated skull, hollowed cheeks, thick lips, and long nose; an outstretch neck, long spindly arms and toothpick legs, the chest of a woman, swollen hips and enormous buttocks; with a large potbelly hanging over his kilt. There has been contention amongst scholars, art scholars, and Egyptologists if this depiction was the genuine look of Amenhotep IV; or as Egyptologist Erik Hornung speculates a "manneristic distortion of reality, a rebellion against the classical idea of beauty."

Some argue if Amenhotep IV was given the position of high priest of Ptah, then he was acting upon the god's namesake: the craftsmen; to which Amenhotep IV was crafting a new art style he believed fitted his new ideal philosophy. We can see this with plaques of the Aten on the stomach and chest. If this is true, then why did he wish to portray himself with feminine features?

From his point of view, the Aten contained both male and feminine qualities that allows it to create life from its life-

**Amenhotep IV's new look (18th Dynasty) housed at the Cairo Museum**

Statue of Amenhotep IV. Notice the spindly arms, the pot belly
over the kilt, and the elongated skull. Located at the Rosicrucian
Museum, San Jose, CA

**Remains of Amenhotep IV statue (18th dynasty) located at the Cairo Museum**

giving rays. If it is true Amenhotep IV was crafting a new art style, then he deemed it a necessity to be depicted encompassing these features- as a form of devotion to the Aten as a universal god- yet it's not out of the realm of possibility that this depiction could be an authentic look at Amenhotep IV. If not, then this was a show de force of Amenhotep IV's artistic creativity at work.

**Wall reliefs remains from *Gempaaten* (18<sup>th</sup> Dynasty)**

## Co-Regency with the Aten

In Year 3, Amenhotep IV decided to hold his first **Sed Festival**. Egyptologists and scholars were perplexed as to why Amenhotep IV decided to have his Sed Festival so early on. Traditionally, the Sed Festivals were to be held on the pharaoh's thirtieth year on the throne was a physical test to prove the pharaoh was still strong to lead and to reassert the pharaoh's right to rule. Amenhotep IV may have been too impatient to wait or like any person with wealth and power, wanted to spend it on a grand party; however, it's very likely this was part of his plan to have his first jubilee at *Gempaaten*.

By having the sed festival at *Gempaaten*, Amenhotep IV outlawed Amun and the other gods from worship. Once the festivities began, Amenhotep IV announced to his guests his jubilee wasn't solely about proving his physical might to the gods but was for new personal god, the Aten. To compound matters, Amenhotep IV made a bold statement that after the death of his father, he had transformed himself to the Aten itself. Now, as the Aten, the once glorious reign of Amenhotep III could continue for eons to come through yearly sed festivals, but Amenhotep IV wasn't done. He made an audacious claim since his father had become the Aten, he himself was a god.

To close out the festivities, Amenhotep IV proclaimed he and the Aten would co-rule as joint sovereigns as he refers to the Aten as '*Re-Horakhti, who rejoices in the horizon in his name Shu, who is the Aten.*' This Sed Festival at *Gempaaten* marked the beginning of Amenhotep IV's master plan. In an insult towards the priests of Amun, he decreed he would act as the Aten's high priest and would spend majority of his worship at *Gempaaten*. Whether Amenhotep IV knew of the corruption is up for debate, but it's possible he may have known there was corruption. Before the year was up, Amenhotep IV had placed the Aten's name in a cartouche alongside his own- a first for any god in Egypt- but Amenhotep IV would take his co-regency with the Aten to a whole new level.

Modern wall relief of Amenhotep IV presenting his offering before the Aten. Rosicrucian Museum, San Jose, CA.

# 7

# The Ascension of Akhenaten

Although Amenhotep IV believed everything went well at his first sed festival, it couldn't be further from the truth. When the people found out Amun and all subsequent gods were outlawed from the now yearly sed festivals, they were livid. On one hand, there were loyal acolytes who praised Amenhotep IV's decision, the wave of foreigners who saw it as the pharaoh recognizing their autonomy and worship; however, regular Egyptians felt betrayed by their pharaoh- forbidding the procession of the gods and be forced to accept it with not question. Every priest in Egypt- including the high priest of Amun- deemed Amenhotep IV's action as an attack not only on Maat but their livelihood.

If this is true, then why didn't the high priest of Amun or any priest for that matter, tried to seize power away from (in their eyes) and incompetent pharaoh? Their decision to call out Amenhotep IV for his actions could've changed the course of the Eighteenth Dynasty, but they didn't. In fact, they didn't really do anything to stop what was about to come. We don't

**Fragment of Amenhotep IV and the Aten (18th Dynasty).**

know if the priests did do something- and if there were any record of their attempt to attack the pharaoh then it was either destroyed or never happened- yet, if the high priest of Amun-Ra had decided to flex their abundant political, religious, and economic power onto Amenhotep IV, the consequences would've been disastrous.

For starters, the priests could've bribed the pharaoh's brothers with more gold than the pharaoh gives them and convince them to join their side and lead a coup d'état on the pharaoh; or conscripted their own army and overthrow the pharaoh themselves. If that happened, then territories subjugated by Egypt would see this a beacon to rebel against their Egyptian overlord, but an event like this wouldn't transpire until the tail end of the New Kingdom- when the government and economy was generally weaken due to foreign invaders from the sea-called the Sea People cutting Egypt from its Near East territory. This action resulted in the Third Intermediate Period (1069-525 BC) seeing a decentralized Egypt ruled by these hereditary priests.

Whatever the case maybe- whether it was fate or luck- the priests didn't attack Amenhotep IV-which would come back to bite them for what was about to come next. If Amenhotep III was trying to subvert power away from the priests, then Amenhotep IV was doing everything in his power to destroy them.

## Call from The Aten

Amun-Ra at his sed festivals, must've taxed the young Amenhotep IV's mind. Going to *Gempaaten* every day alone was a nightmare for Amenhotep IV; those who saw him would lash out at him and try to get a piece of him. Whats worse, his beloved *Gempaaten* was overshadowed by the cult of Amun itself. Just being close to Ipetsut made *Gempaaten* look like an eye sore. Having the Aten there was a constant reminder for Amenhotep IV that Amun had complete hegemony over him. If the Aten cult was to stand on its own, then it would need a domain untouched by any other god but was there such a place for the Aten in Egypt?

Every day, Amenhotep IV would visit the temple pleading to the Aten to show him a domain free from Amun and the gods, where they could rule together. One day, in his frustration, Amenhotep IV took up his chariot, and stormed off into the desert. As he rode north, the felt something was calling out to him to keep going in the same direction. Answering the call, Amenhotep IV kept riding north until the feeling seized and as he stopped, the pharaoh gazed at limestone cliffs towering over a seven-mile-long- and three miles wide strip- of endless desert.

This spot, known as **Middle Egypt**, was located on the eastern bank of the Nile, and was sandwiched between the administrative capital Memphis and the center for the cult of Amun at Thebes. The plain itself was secluded with the towering cliffs acting as an impenetrable shield against invaders. What made Amenhotep IV ecstatic the most was the land was pure and untouched by Amun or any gods because the cliffs itself formed the hieroglyphic symbol for horizon. This site seemed to be tailored made for the Aten!

Although the site the Aten had chosen for Amenhotep IV was an ideal choice, there was the issue of temperature. Due to its location, the area was extremely hot and possibly uninhabitable. You would have to be a mad man to live in this area; but Amenhotep IV was a visionary. He envisioned not just a new temple complex for the Aten, but an entirely new city. Before returning to Thebes, Amenhotep IV name this deserted site as **Akhetaten (‘***the horizon of the Aten***’)** as not only the birthplace of the Aten but the world.

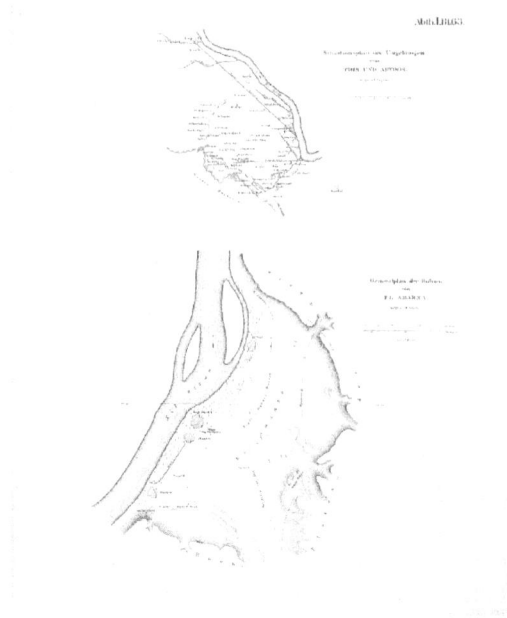

**Map of the future site of Akhetaten (19th century)**

## Amenhotep IV's Vision for Egypt

In Year 5, Amenhotep returned to Akhetaten, only this time he brought along with him his royal courtiers to join him. As the courtiers awaited for the arrival of the pharaoh- and not trying to get burned under the blazing sun- Amenhotep IV appeared before his courtiers in a dazzling golden electrum chariot. The chariot represented the rays of the Aten with Akhenaten embodying the manifestation of the Aten. Amenhotep IV told his courtiers the reason he dragged them to Akhetaten was to show them his plan-he has been working on -for the future of Egypt. Amenhotep IV proclaimed Akhetaten would not only be

Egypt's new capital but the city itself would be the largest
temple complex Egypt had ever seen. Amenhotep IV's plan
would be etched for prosperity on a Boundary Stele A located
on Akhetaten's eastern cliffs:

'As the Aten is beheld, the Aten desires that there be made
for him…as a monument with an eternal and everlasting
name. Now, it is the Aten, my father, who advised me
concerning it,[namely] Akhetaten. No official has ever
advised me concerning it, not any of the people where are
in the entire land has ever advised me concerning it, to
suggest making Akhetaten in this distant place. It was the
Aten, my fath[er who advised me] concerning it, so that it
might be made for him as Akhetaten….

Behold, it is Pharaoh who has discovered it: not being the
property of a god, not being the property of a goddess, not
being the property of a ruler ,not being a property of a
female ruler, not being the property of any people to lay
claim to it….'

According to stele, Amenhotep IV claims the Aten had
personally directed him to Akhetaten- something no other god
had done. But once more, we see Amenhotep IV kept his word
about his father as the Aten and we can see this as one of
Amenhotep IV's plans. Why? Since Amenhotep III was now

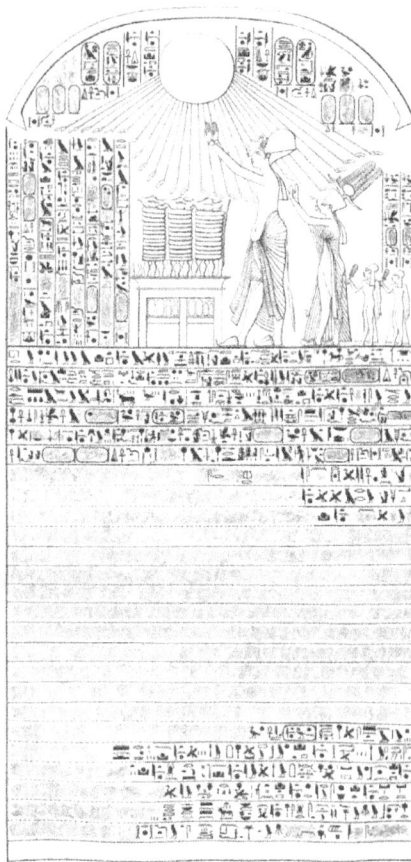

**Sketch of Boundary Stele A (19ᵗʰ Century/18ᵗʰ Dynasty)**

**Sketch of Boundary Stele U (19th Century/18th Dynasty)**

the Aten, his choice of where Akhetaten should be built to be his will and accept his decision to be good for Egypt. Amenhotep IV further elaborates it was, he, who founded the city- this could've been Amenhotep IV fueling his own ego or asserting the power his co-regency he had with the Aten.

As he spoke, Amenhotep IV led his courtiers to an open altar - where the Aten's grand temple was to be built- and made an open air offering before the Aten. Here, Amenhotep IV addressed his planned layout of Akhetaten:

'I shall make Akhetaten for the Aten, my father, in this place. I shall not make Akhetaten for him to the south of it, to the north of it, to the west of it, to the east of it. I shall not expand beyond the southern stela of Akhetaten toward the south, nor shall I expand beyond the northern stela of Akhetaten toward the north, in order to make Akhetaten for him there. Nor shall I make [it] for him on the western side of Akhetaten, but I shall make Akhetaten for the Aten, my father, on the east of Akhetaten, the place that he himself made to be enclosed for him by the mountain...'

Today, you can see Amenhotep IV's plan for the city's limits by a series of carved steles on Akhetaten's eastern and western cliffs. Amenhotep IV further elaborates Akhetaten wouldn't be just any old city, but one big temple dedicated only to the Aten and no other cult:

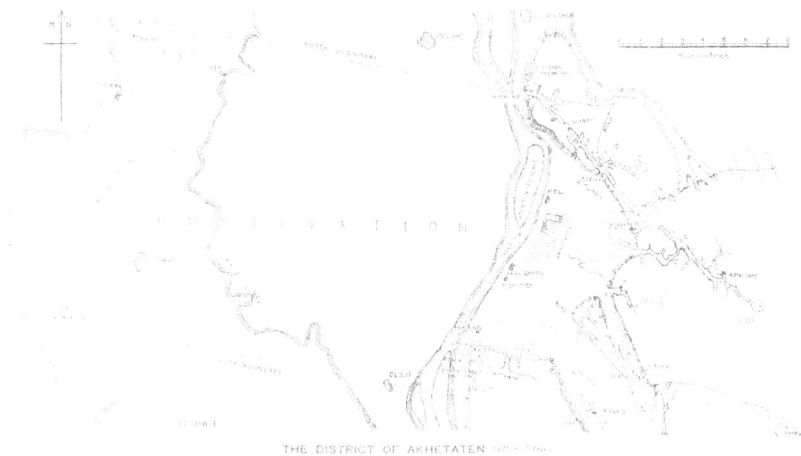

**Layout of the city through the Boundary Steles.**

'I shall make the 'House of the Aten' for the Aten, my
father, in Akhetaten in this place. I shall make the
Mansion of the Aten' for the Aten, my father, in Akhetaten
in this place. I shall make the Sun-Temple…for the Aten, my
father, in Akhetaten in this place I shall make the 'House of
Rejoicing' for the Aten, my father in the Island of the Aten,
Distinguished in Jubilees in Akhetaten in this place….

Once more, Amenhotep IV outlawed Amun and the gods from
touching the ground where the Aten's rays touched. He even
goes as far as stating Akhetaten would be the site he would be
buried:

'Let a tomb be made for me in the eastern mountain [ of Akhetaten]. Let my burial be made in it, in the millions of jubilees that the Aten, my father, has decreed for me...if I die in any town downstream, to the south, to the west or the east in three millions of years, let me brought back so that I may be buried in Akhetaten.'

By being buried in the eastern cliffs, Amenhotep IV plans for his mummified body to be continuously blessed and renewed by the Aten's life-giving rays for eons to come.

Although his royal courtiers were "in favor" of their pharaoh's proclamation, they failed to realize Amenhotep IV was setting the stage to sever his ties completely from Egypt's polytheistic (meaning the worship of one or more) religion; in favor for one based on monotheism (meaning the worship of only one)..

## Silencing the Gods

With his future planned out and new utopia secured, it was time for Amenhotep IV to finish what his father had failed to do: destroying the priesthood. In Year 5, at a private meeting, Amenhotep IV addressed his courtiers his new plan to free Egypt from decades of corruption and decadence. He proclaimed it was once the pharaoh's sacred duty to uphold the will of Maat (the truth and the universe); however, since he was the son of the Aten, he was the living embodiment of Maat.

In his eyes, Amenhotep IV saw it within him his word should be treated as absolute truth; to which everyone must accept it as fact. At the end the of meeting, Amenhotep IV announced in order to make his plans for Akhetaten a reality, he issued a new law to be sent out throughout Egypt: effective immediately, every temple throughout Egypt are to be forcibly shut down:

'Look, I am speaking that I might inform you concerning the forms of the gods. I know their temples and I understand their writings, namely the list of their primeval bodies and I have perceived them as they cease, one after the other, even those consisting of any sort of precious stone…except for the god who made himself from himself.'

Through this one simple speech, Amenhotep IV's plan comes to fruition and ended Egypt's centuries long polytheistic religion. It was at this moment when Amenhotep IV became the first monotheist in recorded history.

## The Birth of *Akhenaten*

To sever his ties completely from the old regime, Amenhotep IV decided to symbolically change his birth to **Akhenaten** ('*effective for the Aten*'). Akhenaten believed by changing his name, he was symbolically reborn as a new being created by the Aten. In a cruel and liberating fashion, Akhenaten ordered his masons to remove Amenhotep IV from every wall, temple, statues, steles across Egypt and replace it with his true name. In a final insult, Akhenaten had the Amun suffix forcibly etched out from Amenhotep III's name and leave it as Hotep III. This signified Amenhotep III was no longer tied to Amun but to the Dazzling Orb and the creator of the universe. Across

Blue turquoise seal ring with the name of Akhenaten. 18th Dynasty (top). Mold containing the cartouche of Akhenaten. 18th Dynasty (bottom).

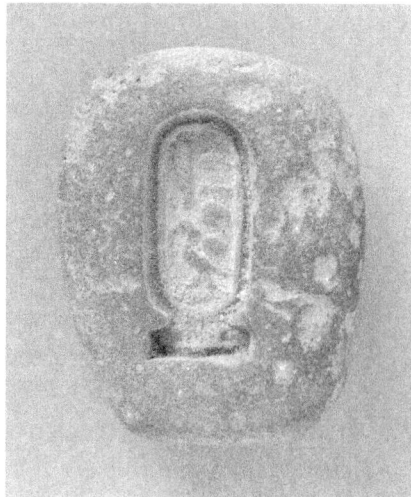

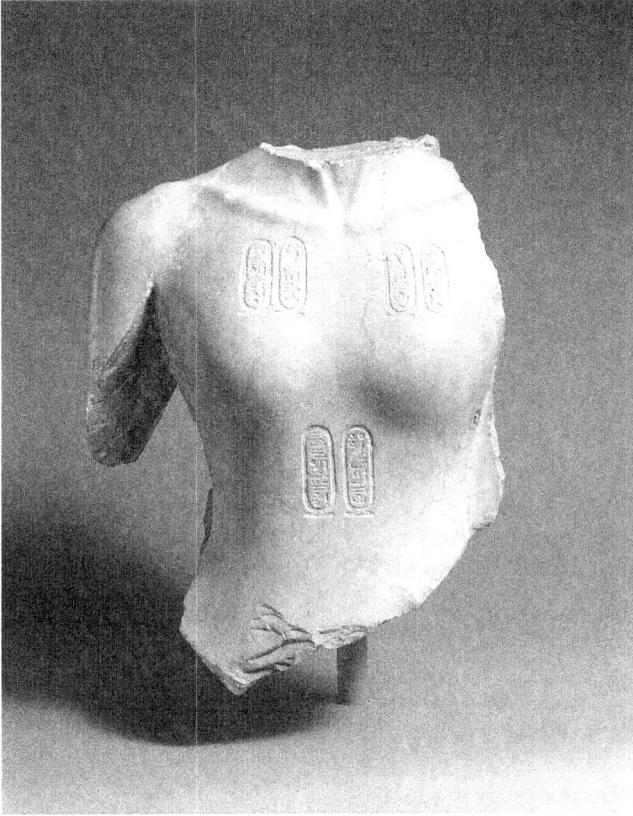

**Torso containing the cartouches of Akhenaten and the Aten (18th Dynasty)**

**Sculpt head of Akhenaten (18ᵗʰ Dynasty)**

Egypt, every temple shut their doors leaving every priest and high priest penniless, powerless, and destitute.

It's ironic, with all the power they had at their disposal, they could have claimed Egypt for themselves, yet they failed to stop a "pretender" to the trhone. With his enemies stripped of their power and income, Akhenaten was now free to reshape Egypt and the world in the image of the Aten.

# 8

## Akhetaten

With the temples closed, the priest hood left destitute, and the funds to build Akhetaten, Akhenaten was now ready to bring his utopia to life. It's unclear if any courtier within Akhenaten's court tried to convince him to reconsider his decision. After all, the Egyptian people were already unhappy few years prior and now they had to contend with the gods being closed off to them was too much. But what is clear, every plan Akhenaten had planned was finally coming to fruition. He could now begin spreading his new inclusive cult of the Aten.

In Year 6, Akhenaten returned to Akhetaten for a second time to inspect the city's progress but made sure his architects were methodically following his plans from the temples to homes, be open to the Aten. As soon as he arrived, Akhenaten would've been bombarded by the blistering sun, the defiant yells of overseers to the workers to work faster- as the workers carried bricks to the site where the Aten's new temple would stand. To escape the unforgiving heat, Akhenaten had his own personal

**Sketch of Boundary Stele S (19ᵗʰ Century/18ᵗʰ Dynasty)**

tent, '*the Aten is content,*' where he would spend his time going over his plans for the city's future and his regime.

While staying in his tent, Akhenaten had an altar placed to make a new offering to the Aten; swearing to him Akhetaten would forever belong to not only him but to his loyal son. It was during that same year when Akhenaten ordered eleven new boundary steles to be constructed- which added more to the grueling work they were doing. These new steles reasserted

Akhenaten's oath to loyally serve the Aten. By being at Akhetaten, Akhenaten demanded that work to be sped up and with him there guiding them, would ensure the city to be finished.

It was only during the final touches of the city that Akhenaten ordered the city to be linked together. In his vision for Akhetaten, Akhenaten wanted this link to be called the *Royal Road*. The *Royal Road* ran parallel to the Nile and connected the city's Northern and Southern avenues as the city's "spine". This arduous endeavor eventually paid off in Year 9 when Akhetaten was finally completed.

## Grand Opening

In Year 9, after three years of backbreaking work, Akhenaten was ready to unveil his new utopia to the general populace; however, he didn't just want to unveil Akhetaten to the people, but wanted to fill the city with those loyal to the Aten. Having lived at *Malkata* is entire life, Akhenaten had enough of Thebes and decreed he, his family, and the royal court, would be moving to the herculean city to be with the Aten. The people of Thebes were probably happy the heretic was finally leaving, but Akhenaten wasn't done.

In fact, he decreed that every man, woman, and child had to accompany him as well. Did the people have a say in this matter? Of course not, Akhenaten deemed himself to be the living Maat and if he says he wants everyone to join him at Akhetaten, they had to comply with his word. Unfortunately, we don't know have any written records to show us how they would've felt and if there were any, they are now lost in the

**Sketch from relief of Akhenaten riding into Akhetaten on his golden electrum chariot (19$^{th}$ century/18$^{th}$ Dynasty)**

annals of history. Thousand citizens packed everything they could carry and set out into the desert to make the grueling two-hundred-mile-long trek to Akhetaten; though this travel was wrought with problems the moment they set out.

First, not everyone was traveling on equal terms; those with wealth would take a short cut by traveling up the Nile to make it to the city; while those who are poorer had to take a longer route in the desert. Here, these individuals had to face the unforgiving nature of the sun and hoped they didn't get burnt or die from heat exhaustion and dehydration. After surviving the journey to Akhetaten, the new citizens hoped to be welcomed by Akhenaten, but he was nowhere to be seen.

If going from leaving everything they had behind to walking through the relentless heat was bad enough for these people, imagine now having to wait for Akhenaten under the blistering sun. As they agonizingly stood, what felt like hours than minutes, Akhenaten had finally arrived. Arriving east of the *Royal Road*, Akhenaten- accompanied by loyal guards- stormed the scene on his golden electrum chariot.

Akhenaten would've welcomed them all to their new home and to commemorate this moment, Akhenaten promises a grand party. Before they could celebrate, Akhenaten gave his people a stern warning: if they remain in this city, they are to only worship the Aten and only the Aten. If caught praying to Amun or a different god that wasn't the Aten, they would be severely punished. With that ultimatum in place, the party began. This celebration wasn't just a celebration for the people, but as a demonstration of their power blessing of their new gods the Aten and Akhenaten.

## Central City

In its heyday, Akhetaten's **Central City** acted as the city's administrative district. Before leaving each day, Akhenaten would ride from his palace to his seat in the government back and forth. Why did he do this? This daily chariot ride symbolized the god king Akhenaten not only interacting with his people but as the Aten traversing the city- like the sun disc traverses across the heavens. Within the administrative districts were offices for the royal courtiers, libraries that housed all knowledge and Akhenaten's new philosophies. On the other side, was a headquarter for the local police force called the *Medjay*. Near the far end of the city was Akhenaten's **Great Palace** (*'House of Rejoicing in Akhenaten'*). Although he may have had fond memories of *Malkata*'s solar imagery, Akhenaten wanted to make his palace better than what his father had made.

Designed after *Gempaaten*, the Great Palace was an open court, contained a large courtyard- lined with gigantic statues of Akhenaten himself- while the palace's walls were coated in painted reliefs of the natural world. At the *Great Palace*, Akhenaten received envoys who wished to have an audience with him. Connected to the *Great Palace* was the titular King's House where Akhenaten met his ministers to go over state affairs, but instead of meeting his ministers face to face, Akhenaten would conduct his meetings through the *'Window of Appearance'*.

Seen through numerous reliefs, the *Window of Appearance* depicts Akhenaten appearing before his ministers on the King's House's balcony where he not only listened to his ministers- who were forced to stand in the sun- but showered his loyal followers with collars of gold. At the heart of Central City contained its most defining piece in Akhetaten: **The Great Aten Temple** (*'House of the Aten'*). Linked to the Great Palace by the Royal Road land bridge, the *Great Aten Temple* was the largest solar temple in Egypt. Standing 2,400 ft long and 750 ft wide, the *Great Aten Temple,*

**Sketch of the '*Window of Appearance*'(18<sup>th</sup> Dynasty)**

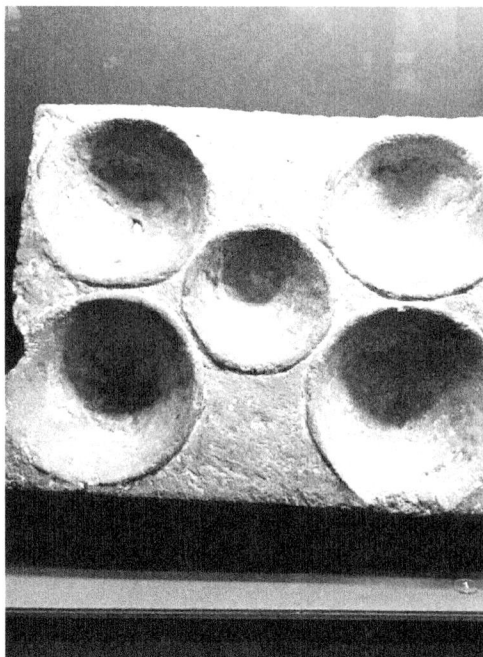

**(Top) Aten Altar. Rosicrucian Museum, San Jose, CA
(Bottom) Relief of Akhenaten being blessed by the Aten**

**Recreation of the opening of Akhetaten.**

like every temple dedicated to the Aten, was open court, contained large mudbrick altars for the Aten's daily offerings. However, in an audacious decree, Akhenaten commissioned three hundred and sixty-five-in astronomical terms, it takes the earth exactly three hundred and sixty-five days to complete its full orbit around the sun- altars to be constructed and distributed up and down the Nile.

Every Egyptian across the country seen at least one of these altars and priests performing offerings before the Aten. Offerings to the Aten were comprised mainly food and wine and had to be made daily so the Aten wouldn't go hungry.

After the priests presented their offerings to the Aten, Akhenaten forbade said priests, the people, and himself to eat and drink until the Aten had its full. Standing beside the altars, were small standing statues of Akhenaten-facing towards the eastern sector of the city. These statues acted as a replacement representation of Akhenaten presenting his own offerings to the Aten-when he failed to make it to the temple. To make it easy for himself, Akhenaten appointed a man named **Meryra** (*'beloved son of Ra'*); for the remainder of Akhenaten's reign, Meryra acted as the Aten's High Priest.

Meryra was given the title of High Priest in Year 9 of Akhenaten's reign. As to who Meryra was, it's believed he was a commoner who became a member of Akhenaten's close inner circle of acolytes and received favoritism from the sun pharaoh. He would go on to receive a special reward from Akhenaten- due to his unbreakable loyalty to the pharaoh- known as the *'gold of honor'* the highest achievement for any commoner in Egypt. In this ceremony, Meryra was blessed with heavy collared beads made entirely from gold from Akhenaten- as he raised his arms to present his own worship of Akhenaten.

Further south from the *Great Aten Temple* was a smaller temple known as the **Small Aten Temple** (*'Mansion of the Aten'*). The *Small Aten Temple* resembled less of a temple and more like a fortress than a temple- on the temple's rooftops, contained its own armory- and was constructed as a single subdivided building. Despite containing stone pylons, the *Small Aten Temple's* walls were coated with images of the Aten blessing Akhenaten as he celebrates his victories over his enemies; however, the *Small Aten Temple* was Akhenaten's own Mortuary Temple, but with a twist. Instead of celebrating the pharaoh before and after death, Akhenaten's temple served to celebrate himself every day' as the Great Temple renews the Small Temple with its life-giving rays.

## North City

Towards the Royal Road's northern end was Akhetaten's **North City**. Referred to as Akhetaten's business district, *North City* had its own administrative complex, but unlike *Central City*'s heavily administrative district, North City housed warehouses and storerooms for the workers. Within in the city's southern end was **The Northern Suburb**; where the elite class, courtiers, and the priests of Akhetaten live in large well-furnished villas. Towards the city's western end was the squared **North Riverside Palace** and was probably the home of Akhenaten.

The North Palace is well known today for its beautifully decorated reliefs of marsh life but had the distinction of serving as the household for Akhenaten's wife and their children. If the *Northern Suburb* contained beautiful, decorated villas, then the city's **Southern Suburb** housed Akhenaten's most important advisers. Unlike Akhenaten's, whose villa was detached from the general populace, the Southern Suburb housed Akhenaten's loyal priests, **Pawah**, his vizier **Nakht**, commander of the armed forces **Ramose** and his chief sculptor ironically named **Thutmose**. These individuals who were loyal to Akhenaten had the privilege to live a life of luxury akin to Akhenaten himself; such as living in open courted villas surrounded by lavish beautiful gardens, ornamental ponds littered with water

Great Pavement from the Northern Palace (18th Dynasty)

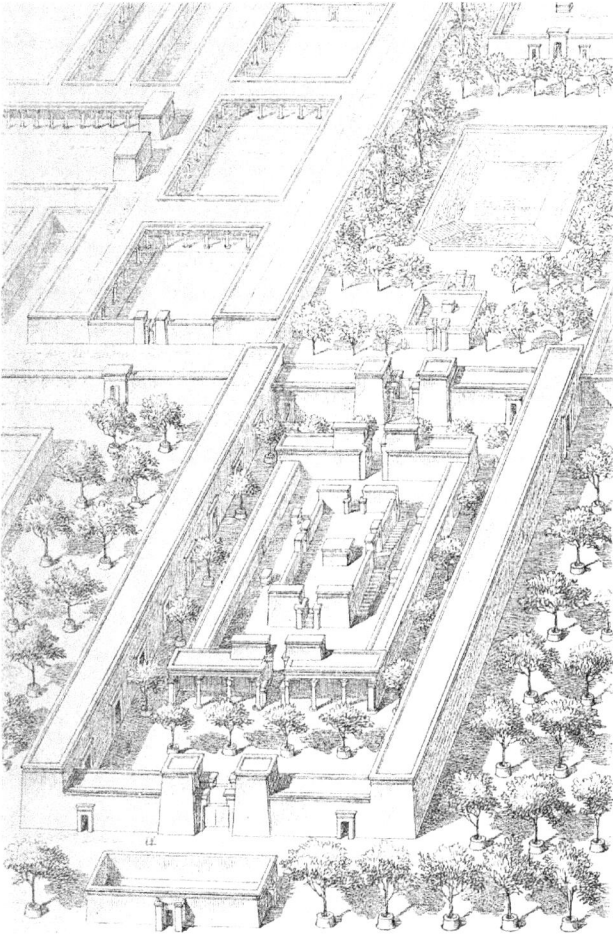

**Layout of Akhetaten**

Section through V. 37. 1

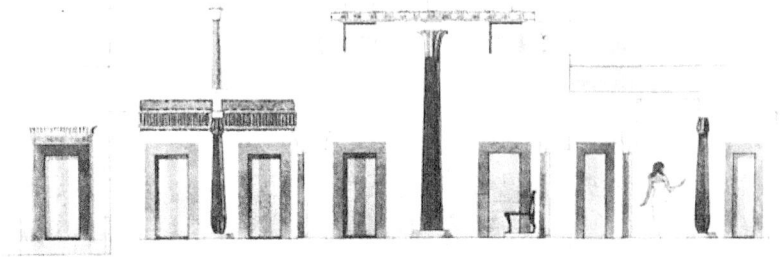

**Villas of Akhetaten. Rosicrucian Museum, San Jose, CA**

lilies and fish; while the villas interiors were well furnished, had fireplaces, bedrooms, and even toilets.

Further away from the main villas- but still on the main property- were the servant quarters, granaries, workshops, storehouses, and wells; they tended the needs of the home, yet they were part of the city's lower class. To demonstrate the difference of power amongst the people, Akhenaten had ordered an enormous wall to be built. What is the significance

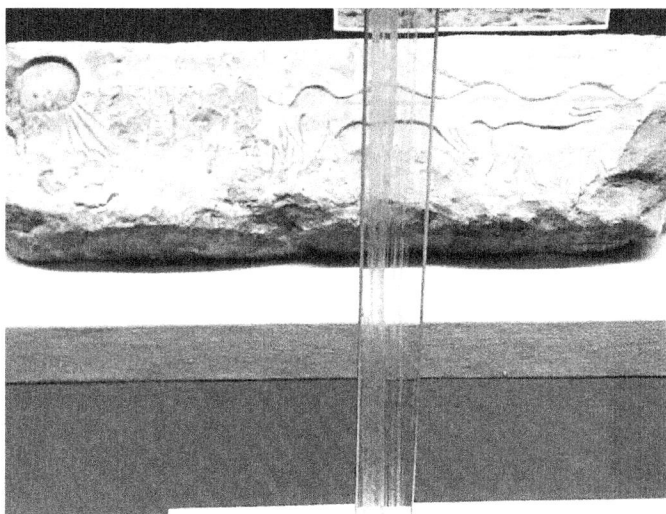

**The Aten blessing nature with its life-giving rays. From Akhetaten, 18th dynasty. Located today at the Rosicrucian Museum, San Jose, CA; Scene from Akhetaten (bottom) 18th Dynasty**

of this? Akhenaten wanted his loyal followers to live their lives in luxury, yet the real reason he wanted this wall built was to keep potential thieves crossing over and separating the rich from the poor- so the nobility could enjoy their privacy.

Unfortunately for those living outside the wall, were amongst the poorer class of Akhetaten. Besides being extremely loud, the streets were uncomfortably cramped, dirty, and vile. Those who were lucky to have a home got the bare bones: these homes were smaller, barely furnished, and were either coated with one lifeless or bland whitewashed color.

## International Appeal

As soon as Akhetaten was open to the world, word began spreading throughout the Mediterranean of the most beautiful gardens they have ever seen; ponds so rich with fish, with the city's walls covered in highly decorated reliefs of the natural world in action. With a population of fifty thousand, Akhetaten became a new metropolitan city the ancient world couldn't get enough of! Soon after, many foreigners and dignitaries from the Near East- and even as far as the Aegean Sea- made their own trek to Akhetaten to gander at the city's beauty and wonder. There were visitors who loved being at Akhetaten so much so, they decided to live amongst Akhenaten and the Aten's life-giving rays. Even the elderly Queen Tiye would stop by from time to time to visit Akhenaten and her grandchildren. As he gazed at the new world he created with the Aten, Akhenaten couldn't have imagine accomplishing his dream if it weren't for his partner to whom he deemed as the 'Great Love of His Life,' yet the world would come to know her as the ideal image of beauty.

# 9

# Queen Nefertiti

December 6, 1912. It had been two decades since Petrie lead the first excavation at Akhetaten; now, a new team funded by the *Deutsche Orient-Gessellschaft* (German Oriental Society) tasked noteworthy Egyptologist Ludwig Borchardt to find new discoveries trapped within the sands of Akhetaten. Unfortunately for the *German Oriental Society*, Borchardt had failed to discover any remains, but that didn't stop Borchardt to keep looking. One day, as he was glancing over documents, Borchardt was interrupted by an Arab worker who claimed they had discovered something big.

Borchardt quickly rushed out of his tent to where the workers were slowly unearthing what appeared to be a human face. After ordering his workers to stand aside, Borchardt took out a small brush and as he brushed the hot sands from the face, the stone face stared back at him and in turn stared back at him.

For Borchardt, this was the most beautiful face he had ever seen in his life; however, this wasn't just an ordinary pretty face. This was a face of Egypt's greatest queens: **Nefertiti**.

**Portrait of Ludwig Borchardt (19th Century)**

Borchardt then ordered the workers to carefully remove the face from the earth, but as they lifted the face, Borchardt was shocked to discover this face wasn't a broken piece, but an entire sculpture. After cleaning the statue from centuries of sand, the sculpture was just as beautiful as the face bearing it: made from limestone, the face was symmetrical with fair olive brownish skin, an exaggerated long slender neck, rose colored lips-conveying a warm smile- almond shaped eyes, long black arch eyebrows; while a long blue, red and green beaded collar rested gently on her clavicle. To top it off, the sculpture had a large flat-topped blue crown adorned with golden ribbons and golden uraeus (cobra) stationed on her head.

Although the sculpture was intact and in good shape, there were some noticeable damages such as missing a large piece of her ear, the golden uraeus broken off hasn't been discovered since- and her left eye is missing from her socket. But, despite the minor abnormalities, didn't hinder the significance of the find.

Unbeknownst to Borchardt, the site where he unearthed the sculpture was directly on top of what used to be the workshop of Akhetaten's chief sculptor, **Thutmose**. It's agreed upon by Egyptologists the sculpture, at some point in the past, was placed on a wooden shelf, but when the city was abandoned, the wood shelf rotted causing the sculpture to hit the ground and as centuries went on, the sands pushed the sculpture up till it was eye level.

Before turning in for the night, Borchardt wrote only one sentence in his diary: "Description is useless, see for yourself." After the winter season had ended, Borchardt secretly smuggled the sculpture out of Egypt and brought it back to Berlin as a gift to his benefactors. From there, the sculpture would be put on display for the world to gaze in 1924 at Berlin's **Agyptisches Museum**; however, Egypt's antiquities services have tried and failed to reclaim the sculpture- which they deemed to be illegally stolen from Borchardt. So, who was the real Nefertiti behind the sculpture? What role did she play in Akhenaten's plans?

## Royalty? Commoner? Or Foreign Princess?

By the time Akhenaten had ascended to the throne in 1353 BC, he was already married to Nefertiti, yet we know so little of her

The bust of Queen Nefertiti. Though perfectly intact, it's missing the golden uraeus, piece of her left ear, and left eye. Located today at the Agyptisches Museum, Berlin.

**Painting of Thutmose sculpting the bust of Nefertiti as the queen sits and remains motionless. Located at the Rosicrucian Museum, San Jose, CA.**

life before she was jettison to prominence. Like Akhenaten, Nefertiti's life is a jigsaw puzzle, but unlike Akhenaten, we are missing even more pieces of her life. Egyptologists for the longest time had painstakingly tried to piece together who Nefertiti's parents were. There are those who claim Nefertiti wasn't Egyptian due to her name (*'A Beautiful Woman Has Come'*) and was instead Mitanni princess **Tadukhepa**- sent to Egypt during Amenhotep III's reign. Others claim Nefertiti

**Akhenaten and Nefertiti. From the ruins at Akhetaten. 18th Dynasty**

was a commoner and the marriage between Akhenaten and Nefertiti would break Egyptian custom.

 However, Egyptologists on the opposing side have tossed these theories out and instead lean towards Nefertiti having a sister named **Mutnodjmet** and was probably the daughter of Akhenaten's vizier, **Aye** and his unknown wife but was raised by Aye's second wife, **Tey**-who claims to be 'nurse of the king's great wife Nefertiti, nurse of the goddess, ornament of the pharaoh'. If this is true, then this means Akhenaten's mother, Tiye, was her aunt; making Nefertiti Akhenaten's first cousin- meaning Akhenaten was continuing the tradition of marrying within the family.

In Egyptian custom, it was mandated when the pharaoh was selecting his queen, he should be pick from within the royal family- these family members could be cousins or sisters. Why would the Egyptians practice this taboo method? Though we see this as an act of taboo, back then it was fully accepted by Egyptians; they believed the union between blooded relatives meant their children would have double divine blood ensuring their legitimacy to the throne. This means, Akhenaten and Nefertiti's children would have the same double divine blood.

If Nefertiti is the daughter of Aye, then she grew up alongside Akhenaten, and probably was the one person Akhenaten trusted alongside his mother. As she got older, Akhenaten would choose Nefertiti as his wife and once marrying Akhenaten, Nefertiti would find herself married to a formidable idealist; whose plans was to reshape Egypt through his obsession with the Aten and found herself dragged into his obsession.

## Role in the New Religion

During the construction of *Gempaaten*-when Akhenaten was still Amenhotep IV- Amenhotep IV commissioned a second subsidiary temple to be constructed alongside the temple. This smaller temple, **Hwt-Benben** (*'Mansion of the Benben Stone'*),

Relief of Akhenaten and Nefertiti presenting their offerings to the Aten. It was essential for both parties to be present when making offerings before the Aten (18th Dynasty)

**(Top/Bottom) Cartouches containing the names of Nefertiti**

too was an open court but acted as the feminine counterpart to the masculine *Gempaaten*. Hwt-Benben's columns were covered in gargantuan statues of Nefertiti portrayed in the same exaggerated features as Akhenaten- to demonstrate that even the queen contained both masculine and feminine features- but Hwt-Benben served a secondary purpose.

Although remnants of Hwt-Benben lie in only blocks of wall reliefs, it's within these remains that Egyptologists discovered scenes of Nefertiti, her daughter, shaking sistrums (Egyptian rattler) beneath the Aten's life-giving rays while Akhenaten presents offerings; however, there was another relief of Nefertiti presenting her offerings to the Aten. Why was Nefertiti allowed to make offerings before the Aten?? Whenever Nefertiti was depicted alongside Akhenaten, she was to be presented as his subsidiary while he presented his offerings to the Aten, but, at Hwt-Benben, Nefertiti would take the position of pharaoh while their daughter becomes Nefertiti's queen.

In Akhenaten's philosophy, the Aten cannot be satisfied by the pharaoh himself, but both the pharaoh and queen need to be present when the offerings are made. This new ideology gave the queen exceptional power to that of the pharaoh. In his eyes, the queen was his true equal. This equality goes beyond wall reliefs. When Akhenaten was too busy to perform his daily rituals for the Aten; Nefertiti and their daughter would go to *Gempaaten* and perform the ritual.

At his first sed festival, Akhenaten decreed his father was the living embodiment of the Aten (Ra), but Akhenaten took it one step further by proclaiming himself and Nefertiti as the gods

**Cartouche of Neferneferuaten (18ᵗʰ Dynasty)**

Shu and Tefnut. We have seen this proclamation before (subtly) with Akhenaten's statues at *Gempaaten* sporting Shu's signature two plums on top of his nemes headdress. In Egyptian mythology, Ra, Shu, and Tefnut were the Egyptian triad with Shu (*'He who rises up'*) and Tefnut (*'The Eye of Ra'*) being the children of Ra; each being an eye of Ra.

When Amenhotep IV changed his name to Akhenaten in Year 5, Akhenaten gave Nefertiti an additional name **Neferneferuaten** (*'Perfect One of Aten's Perfection'*) with her cartouche bearing the Aten- only it was reversed facing her name to indicate Nefertiti being the first queen to be allowed to "gaze" at the Aten.

## Queenly Role

When it came to her role as Egypt's queen, Nefertiti was given exceptional power by Akhenaten. One practice Akhenaten continued from his father was making the queen his true equal. She was given the distinguished feminine title *'Lady of the Two Lands'* to go alongside Akhenaten's masculine *'Lord of the Two Lands'*. Together, they would be equals in power and status. A great example of this equality can be seen from recovered wall reliefs at Karnak and Heliopolis.

In these depictions shows Nefertiti behind Akhenaten as he delivers the finishing blow to his enemies under the Aten; with a secondary depiction of Nefertiti- with her daughter standing behind her- taking on the role as pharaoh and smiting Egypt's enemies as well. This reinforces Akhenaten's philosophy of the Aten not only needing both Nefertiti and Akhenaten to be present in any affair- either religious or political means- to be satisfied but as a warning to Egypt's enemies their queen was just as powerful as the pharaoh.

In Year 5, Nefertiti and their daughter accompanied Akhenaten to Akhetaten. During this time, when Akhenaten commissioned steles as markers for the city's limits, had Nefertiti to be constructed right next to them as a founder as well. Akhenaten even goes to great length of the importance of how Nefertiti and their daughter were essential to the new religion:

**Fragment containing the names of the Aten, Akhenaten, and
Nefertiti (18ᵗʰ Dynasty)**

'I shall make the Sun-Temple of the [Great King's] Wife
[Neferneferuaten-Nefertiti] for the Aten, my father, in
Akhetaten in this place....I shall make for myself the
apartments of Pharaoh, I shall make the apartments of
the Great King's Wife in Akhetaten in this place.... Let
the burial of the Great King's Wife, Nefertiti, be made in it,
in the millions of ye[ars that the Aten, my father decreed, for
her. Let the burial of] the King's Daughter, Merytaten,
[be made] in it, in these millions of years....

If the Great King's Wife, Nefertiti dies in any town downstream, to the south, to the west, to the east in these millions [of years, let her be brought back, that] she [may be buried in Akhetaten. If the King's Daughter, Meryetaten, dies] in any town downstream, to the south, to the west, to the east in these millions of years, let her be brought back, that [she] may be buried in Akhetaten.'

Nefertiti would return with Akhenaten the following year as construction of the city was underway. Once Akhetaten was completed in Year 9, Akhenaten had named Nefertiti his co-regent, but why would he name her his co-regent?

Egyptologists have theorized Akhenaten's new ideology was vulnerable to be undone if he were to die- and wanted to spend more time refining the Aten religion. So, to rectify this problem, it made sense for Akhenaten to name Nefertiti as his co-regent: she knew all the rituals, policies, and would be able to continue the cult of the Aten when he passes. Akhenaten trusted Nefertiti to continue carrying out his philosophical ideology. This in turn made their co-regency to be split into two but still equal parts: Nefertiti would take on the political role as she oversees the Egyptian government- to whom the courtiers would've trusted with the decision making- while Akhenaten closes himself from Egypt (and the world) by residing in Akhetaten and obsessing over the Aten. As such, their co-regency was co-dependent on one another to keep the cult of the Aten flourishing for eons.

## Family Life

Over the course of their marriage, Nefertiti would bear Akhenaten six daughters. Their first daughter, **Meretaten**

(Top) Akhenaten and Nefertiti in loving embrace. Sketched in 1893, Akhetaten.

**(Left to Right) Meretaten (holding the sistrums), Nefertiti, and Akhenaten (18ᵗʰ Dynasty)**

would be born right a year after Amenhotep IV and Nefertiti got married. As the first born of a new dynasty, Meretaten given just as much power as her mother; something not seen in this period, but Akhenaten deemed it to be so that their children be equal in divinity and power. Before the move to Akhetaten,

Fragment containing the names of Akhenaten and three of his daughters (18th Dynasty)

**(Top) Neferneferuaten and Neferneferure. Akhetaten, 18th Dynasty. (Bottom) Three of Akhenaten's daughters. Akhetaten, 18th Dynasty.**

Fragment remain of Nefertiti kissing one of her daughters as the Aten blesses the queen with an ankh. Akhetaten, 18th Dynasty. (Bottom) Nefertiti (as the pharaoh) and Meketaten (face etched off). 18th Dynasty

(Top) Akhenaten and Nefertiti being fanned by their daughters, as the Aten hovers over the pharaoh and queen. Akhetaten, 18th Dynasty. (Bottom) Torso of one of the princesses (18th Dynasty)

Nefertiti would give birth to another daughter, **Meketaten**-who would accompany her older sister to Akhetaten and was even depicted alongside her parents and Meretaten on wall reliefs at Gempaaten and Hwt-Benben.

Their third daughter, **Ankhesenpaaten** (*'May She Live for Aten'*) was born between Akhenaten's sixth and seventh year and she would play a significant role later in life. The latter three, **Neferneferuaten-Tasherit** (*'The Younger'* 1346 BC), **Neferneferure** (*'Perfet One of the Sun's Perfection'* 1345 BC) and finally **Setepenre** (*'She Who the Sun Has Chosen'*); however, what Akhenaten desperately wanted above all else from Nefertiti was a son, but he would get his wish. Although Nefertiti failed to give Akhenaten a son, there was another woman-from amongst Akhenaten's lengthy wives- who bore him a son, **Tutankhaten** (1344 BC), a woman named **Kiya**.

What remains we do have of her depicts her with a sweet face, almond-shaped eyes, and a pretty smile, yet would prove to be one of Akhenaten's favorites; by giving her vast titles such as 'Wife and Great Beloved King of Upper and Lower Egypt Living in Truth, Lord of the Two Lands Neferkheperure Waenre [Akhenaten], the perfect child of the living Aten'.

Akhenaten even went as far as having her participate in rituals for the Aten. It's unknown if Nefertiti would've been jealous of Kiya's new-found place in Akhenaten's life, but Kiya died in 1344 BC- though Egyptologists have failed to come up as to whether she died or disappeared. Even with her disappearance, Akhenaten had Tutankhaten who he could mold into the philosophies of the Aten and be a worthy successor.

During their time in Akhetaten, Nefertiti and Akhenaten would raise their six daughters and Tutankhaten at the North Palace.

Further south of the North Palace was the cult center of **Maru-Aten** a large religious complex for only the women of the royal family and would be an equivalent in power to the Great Aten Temple. Together, Nefertiti, Akhenaten, and their children became the nuclear family of what Egyptologists dubbed this era in Egyptian history as **Amarna Period**, but what did the Amarna Period intel?

# 10

# Art and Religion of the Amarna Period

From the ancient Greeks to the Romans, Egypt's art has captivated generations of artists who would adopt their techniques and are still used today. Although the beauty of Egypt's art continues to inspire many across the world, the art form itself served on its symmetry. To the Egyptians, their art was reflection on the world they lived on and the concept known as Maat (the universe); hence why we referred to their art as symmetry. Maat in Egyptian culture served as the duality between the mortal and divine world; serving as social order in the universe. The Egyptians believed Maat came into existence when the gods emerged from the primordial oceans and created Maat to keep in check the primordial chaos from lashing out.

The gods were the first to introduce the ideas of duality such as day and night, man and woman, land and ocean- given to Maat to regulate. Which is why, when we look at temples, courtyards, gardens, tombs, wall reliefs, statues, we see balance being implemented. For instance, the temple courtyard

**Colossi statue of a Pharaoh. Notice how the figure is emotionless, its left foot placed in front of its right (left represents the heart leading the pharaoh), hands tightly clenched; and is depicted as forever youthful and strong.**

reflected not only Egypt's creation, Maat, the afterlife but *heka* (magic). To many Egyptians, they believed their world was not just a gift given to them by the gods but a reflection of the gods domain. So, when the deceased died and was buried in their tombs, they knew already the place they were going to was just like their home but only better; hence art in Egypt reflected the gods own perfections while serving as a guide in preparing for the afterlife. Despite being admired for their beauty, many critics had criticized Egypt's art styles. For starters, Egyptian art was always two dimensional with static figures- and even the gods to the extent- facing in front of the viewer-depicted emotionless with barely any movement except for one to two arms at a time.

Even statues of the pharaohs and queens seemed to be stuck with the same emotionless expressions; while standing statues of the pharaoh were rigid with their left leg over their right, arms at the sides as their hands clenched into tight ball fists. Despite these claims, the Egyptians understood how emotion worked. They saw emotion as a transition with none either happy or sad or sad to angry; however, they deliberately presented their pieces emotionless so the ka (spirit) could recognize its face in order to make its way to the afterlife.

If they presented the deceased as being angry, the ka wouldn't be able to tell its them, but if the face was emotionless, it would recognize it as his/hers. It was always important for the spirit to recognize its face or its name so it can continue its travel into the afterlife. To the Egyptian people, life in the mortal world was small compared to the bigger journey to the next life.

Their art reflects the importance of death, the need to prepare for the afterlife, and to undergo rebirth in the next world; however, the artwork they left behind tell their life's story, and Egypt's spiritual and cultural values. So, it came a complete surprise to the Egyptian people when Akhenaten systematically decided to forgo centuries of Egyptian art, core values, and reshaped them into his and the Aten's image.

## Amarna Architecture

When he came to power in 1353 BC, Akhenaten decided to radically transform Egypt's art from the ground up. The earliest example came with *Gempaaten* at Luxor when he made the temple opened before the Aten-who would bless the temple complex with its life-giving rays. *Gempaaten's* location was based on an east to western axis as to mirror the Aten's path across the heavens. But how was Akhenaten able to build Gempaaten and Akhetaten in a short period of time? Akhenaten was able to complete his structures through an innovation in architecture called **talatat**. Talatat was first utilized by Amenhotep III as building material for his *Malkata* palace.

Unlike the large limestone blocks cut at the quarry site of Gebel Silsila, talatat were smaller-about the size of the modern brick- entirely made from mudbrick and can easily be carried by one person. Akhenaten benefited greatly using talatat over limestone blocks. Talatats were cheap to make, and could be made by the dozens at a faster rate than having ten workers carving out one limestone block. But this cost saving unfortunately had major drawbacks for Akhenaten. Since the talatats were made entirely from mudbrick, it would degrade at a faster rate over time- unlike limestone which degrades at a much slower rate and can last for thousands of years- which is why the Great Pyramids, and the Sphinx are still around today.

Akhenaten ordered his workers personally to have *Gempaaten*'s wall to be constructed using talatats. He ordered to have the small bricks placed vertically and horizontally. At Akhetaten, the city's vast palaces, statues of Akhenaten and

Nefertiti, and temples were constructed using talatats. Once the bricks were set, any cracks remaining would be filled in with a white plaster. From there, the bricks were coated with a thick layer of white paint for the painters to paint scenes of nature, Akhenaten, the royal family, and the Aten.

## Portrait Style

Amongst the artifacts recovered of Akhenaten, the most striking pieces of art had to be his grotesque portraits. Although his portrait displayed him looking monstrous, it was a welcome change to the emotionless and stiff representation of previous pharaohs. The first artists credited to implement architects for Akhenaten's vision was a man named **Bak**; who oversaw the early depictions of Akhenaten at *Gempaaten*. Akhenaten was an artist and if spending time as High Priest of Ptah during his co-regency with his father is true, then he was implementing Ptah's will as a crafter.

In Akhenaten's eyes, he believed life's realism was the truest art form. At Akhetaten, he encouraged artisans to come to the city to help him develop and modify his new art style. Those who decided to go and dwell in Akhetaten had to forgo centuries of artistic conventions and solely embrace Akhenaten's new art style for the world.

When these artists arrived, Akhenaten would personally teach them all his new ideology for Egyptian art moving forward: to push past artistic conventions, use life and the natural world and imbue them into their art to create a new realism not seen in Egypt. In Akhenaten's later years, he would replace Bak with Thutmose who became an expert in the Amarna style and was in favor of a more relaxed realism than the exaggerated

**(Top/Bottom) Talatat of Akhenaten (18th Dynasty)**

**Elongated Skull of Akhenaten. Akhenaten personally instructed members of the royal family to be depicted with the same skull shape (18th dynasty)**

features Akhenaten wanted to portray. Gone was the image of a young, well fit, and strong pharaoh, now was replaced by weirdly shaped body proportions, and strange elongated skulls. These weird abnormalities made Akhenaten come across not only 'weak" but looked as if he was sick.

For years, Egyptologists had been debating as to why Akhenaten wanted to present himself in this distorted manner. Medical examiners have looked at Akhenaten's depictions and tried to diagnose if he was suffering from a disease. There are those who lean towards **Froehlich's Syndrome** in which the

**Standing statue of Nefertiti. Notice her skull is elongated; while she sports the infused attributes of masculinity and femininity. Located in the Berlin Muesm (18th Dynasty)**

brain's endocrine system is heavily affected; however, Egyptologists disproved this theory. If Akhenaten did have Froehlich's he would be suffering from mental health issues- which caused the individual to be "slow". They lean towards another disease called **Marfan's Syndrome**; where the individual suffered from physical distortions in the arms, the face grows abnormally longer, the ears are deformed, scoliosis (curvature of the spine), and the feminize shape hips, and chest. This diagnosis falls better in line with Akhenaten's depictions, yet many believe Akhenaten wasn't suffering from Froehlich's or Marfans's and was only crafting a new artistic style for the cult of the Aten.

Whatever the case maybe, Akhenaten went as far as having his entire family to be depicted with the same abnormalities, except for Nefertiti. When Nefertiti's bust underwent a CT (Cat) scan for the first time, the examiners discovered underneath the bust's beautiful exterior, showed signs of abnormalities. Under the layers of plaster, the sculpture had a slight bump on the ridge her nose, and wrinkles surrounding around the mouth and cheeks. Many have seen this as the first case of air brushing in history and this was the real Nefertiti. At some point, either Akhenaten or Thutmose decided to change the bust- despite the wrinkles symbolizing Nefertiti as a wise queen- to exemplify her beauty or her godly status.

## Family Representation

In the last chapter, we discussed how Akhenaten declared himself and Nefertiti as the children of the Aten. While living in Akhetaten, Akhenaten decreed their children too were new gods. Before the changes, pharaohs and queens depicted in art were shown as incarnation of the gods and were above the people, but in Akhetaten, it was the exact opposite. Coated on the walls of Akhetaten presented images of daily life of the royal family laughing with one another, Akhenaten and

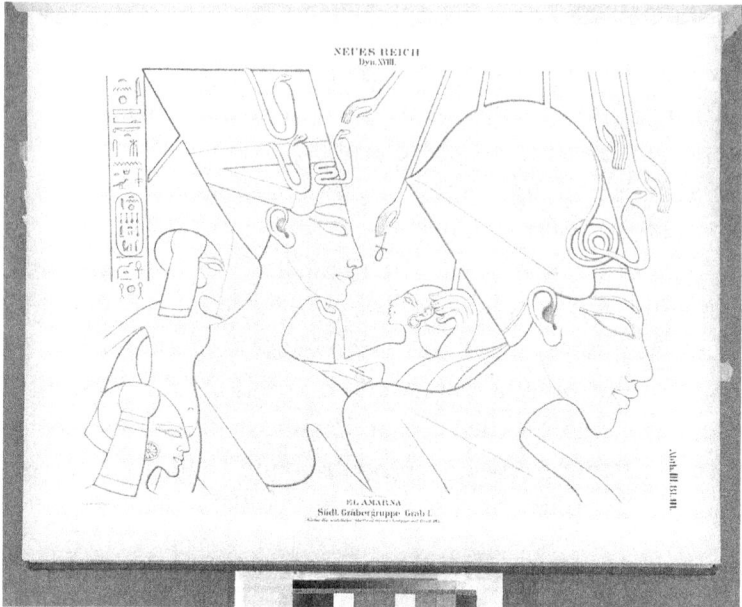

**19th Century Akhenaten, Nefertiti, and their three daughters. Those who lived in the city would see these images plastered on the walls of the city.**

**(Top) Akhenaten and Nefertiti offering to the Aten; as their three daughters play the sistrums. (Bottom) Akhenaten's three daughters**

**Talatat of Akhenaten's daughters (18th Dynasty)**

Nefertiti playing with their daughters- as the Aten's rays blessed the family. These images encompassed Akhenaten's open intimacy for his family and to reinforce the divinity of the royal family as gods.

In every home across Akhetaten, Akhenaten ordered every resident to house shrines displaying miniature statues of Nefertiti and Akhenaten as their gods, yet their divine iconography goes beyond wall reliefs. The royal family had complete control over the citizens of Akhetaten to the extent their prayers to the Aten had to go through Akhenaten, Nefertiti, and their children. Before, Akhenaten decreed he was the mediator to the Aten, but that was when he was still in Thebes; now in his utopia, he decreed Nefertiti and their children to be the mediators to the Aten as well. They even forced the people to kneel outside the 'Window of Appearance' and pray to them, but as they returned home, they still had to contend with their shrines dedicated to Akhenaten and Nefertiti.

This intimacy amongst the royal family didn't stop on the wall reliefs-in fact, there are scenes of the royal families in the tombs of Akhenaten's courtiers. Where once there were images of images of Anubis, Horus, Osiris, and Isis, were replaced by images of the Aten and the royal family. Those who died and buried in Akhetaten's eastern cliffs would have their tomb walls covered by the divine family but were unusually bigger than the figure the tomb belonged to. Even in death, the owners of the tombs were to continue to worship the divine family as gods while the Aten blessed the tomb for the spirits continual rebirth.

## Naturalism and the Great Hymn

Another innovation Akhenaten introduced was the change in depth on flat surfaces. If an image was to be carved or painted on a flat surface, the wall would be covered in a red painted grid, enabling the artist to transfer the static papyrus image onto the wall where they copied the image in red before finishing it with black paint. Once finished, the sculptor carves into the reliefs. From there, the images would be painted. Under Akhenaten's new direction, artists gave more depth to the backgrounds by depicting the Aten and his outstretched hands as expressive- with the image of Akhenaten receiving its blessing being expressive and realistic- and not a still image. Akhenaten instilled his images with realism by allowing the images to express in their faces, the hands and even their body language; opposing he stiff, rigid juxtapose images of the past.

One take away from Akhenaten and the *Amarna Period's* art had to be the depictions of the natural world. Scenes of marsh life shows birds vigorously beating their wings amongst the papyrus, brightly colored fish swimming as the wheat fields sway in the breeze.

This emphasis on the natural world could be linked to Akhenaten's time as a child spending time in the palace gardens, yet it's more likely this emphasis on nature had to do with Akhenaten's philosophy- about the Aten blessing the world with life. In his personal soliloquy for the solar disc called **The Great Hymn to the Aten**. Discovered in the '*tomb of the god's father Ay,*' the Great Hymn is composed into thirteen vertical hieroglyphic columns. Today, the hymn is considered as being "*one of the most significant and splendid pieces of poetry to survive from the pre-Homeric world,*" with some of its verses making its way into the Old Testament of the Bible:


*"Beautifully you appear from the horizon of heaven, O living*

*Aten who initiates life-*

*For you are risen from the eastern horizon and have filled every land with your beauty;*

*For you are fair, great, dazzling and high over every land,*

And your rays enclose the lands to the limits of all you have
made;

For you are Re, having reached their limit and subdued
them for your beloved son;

For although you are far away, your rays are upon the earth
and you are protected.

When your movements vanish and you set in the western

horizon, The land is in darkness, in the manner of death.

People, they lie in bedchambers, heads covered up, and one
eye does not see its fellow.

All their property might be robbed, although it is under
their

heads, and they do not realize it.

Every lion is out of its den, all creeping things bite.

Darkness gathers, the land is silent.

The one who made them is set in his horizon.

But the land grows bright when you are risen from the
horizon,

Shinning in the disc in the daytime, you push back the
darkness and give forth your rays. The Two Lands are in
a festival of light-

*Awake and standing on legs, for you have lifted them up: Their limbs are cleansed and wearing clothes,*

*Their arms are in adoration at your appearing.*

*The whole land, they do the work:*

*All flocks are content with their pasturage,*

*Trees and grasses flourish,*

*Birds are flown from their nests, their wings adorning your ka;*

*All small cattle prance upon their legs.*

*All that fly up and alight, they live when you rise for them.*

*Ships go downstream, and upstream as well, every road being*

*open at your appearance.*

*Fish upon the river leap in front of you, and your rays are even inside the Great Green Sea.*

*O you who brings into being fetuses in women,*

*Who makes fluid in people,*

*Who gives life to the son in his mother's womb, and calms him by stopping his tears;*
*Nurse in the womb, who gives breath to animate all he makes*

*When it descends from the womb to breathe on the day it is born-*

*You open his mouth completely and make what he needs.*

*When the chick is in the egg, speaking in the shell,*

*You give him breath within it to cause him to live;*

*And when you have made his appointed time for him, so that he may break himself out of the egg,*

*He comes out of the egg to speak at his appointed time and goes on his two legs when he comes out of it.*

*How manifold it is, what you have made, although mysterious in the face of humanity,*

*O sole god, without another beside him!*

*You create the earth according to your wish, being alone-*

*People, all large and small animals, All things which are on earth, which go on legs, which rise up and fly by means of their wings,*

*The foreign countries of Kharu [Syria] and Kush [Nubia], and the land of Egypt.*

*You set every man in his place, you make their requirements, each one having his food and the reckoning of his lifetime. Their tongues differ in speech, their natures likewise.*

*Their skins are distinct, for you have made foreigners to be distinct. You make the inundation from the underworld... All for all distant countries, you make their life.*

*You have granted an inundation in heaven, that it might come down for them.*

*And make torrents upon the mountains, like the Great Green (sea), to soak their fields with what suits them....*

*You made heaven far away just to rise in it, to see all you make, Being unique and risen in your aspects of being as 'living Aten'-manifest, shinning, far yet near.*

*You make millions of developments from yourself, you who are a oneness: cities, towns, fields, the path of the river.*

*Every eye observes you in relation to them, for you are Aten of the daytime above the earth....*

*You are in my heart, and there is none who knows you except your son, Neferkheprure-waenre [Akhenaten],*

*For you make him aware of your plans and your strength.*

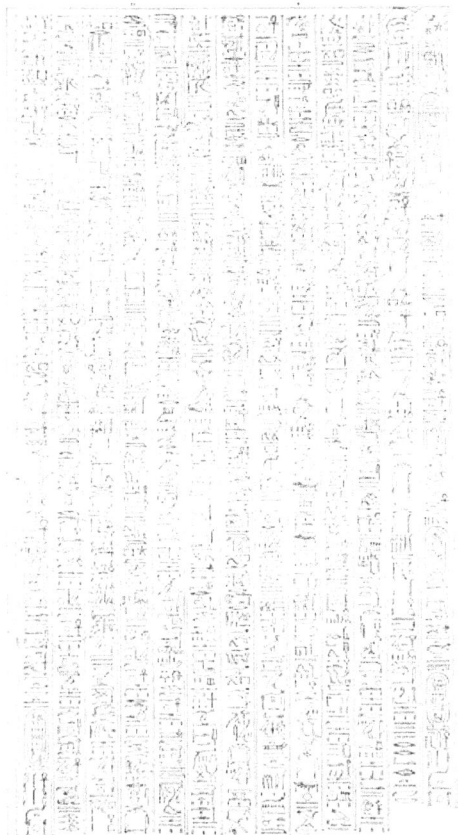

**The Great Hymn to the Aten (18th Dynasty)**

(Top) Female musicians. Notice how expressive and fluid the hands are as they play their instruments ( 18th Dynasty) (Bottom) Stele of Re-Horakhty. Notice how its flat and one dimensional

**Cosmetic dish in the shape of Trussed duck. Amarna art focused on natural life and this dish is one example (18<sup>th</sup> Dynasty)**

*The land develops through your action, just as you made them [people]: When you have risen, they live, but when you set they die. You are lifetime in your very limbs, and one lives by means of you.*

*Until you set, all eyes are upon your beauty but all work is put aside when you set on the western side.*

*You who rise and make all creation grow for the king, as for everyone who hurries about on foot since you founded the land,*

*You raise them up for your son, who issued from your limbs, the king of Upper and Lower Egypt, lives on maat,*

*The lord of the Two Lands, Neferkheprure-waenre,*

*Son of Re, who lives according to maat, lord of diadems,*

*Akhenaten, great in his lifetime...*

Looking at the *Great Hymn* in closer detail, Akhenaten is proclaiming to the world the Aten is the source from where all life stems from. It's the Aten's life-giving rays that gave birth to life in the word-with everything or anyone could receive the blessing of the Aten.

Whether they are plants, animals, the people, or foreigners, they can receive the gift of life from the Aten; however, the

*Great Hymn* served a secondary purpose. This was Akhenaten denying the existence of not only Amun but overall, the gods as well in favor for the Aten. Many Egyptologists concluded the *Great Hymn* as the culmination of the cult of the Aten as entirely monotheistic; however, this would be the last good thing Akhenaten would enjoy as his vision for Egypt was about to fall apart in front of his very eyes.

# 11

# The Fall of Akhenaten

In 1342 BC, Akhenaten decided to hold a magnificent celebration to give thanks to the Aten for all the good he's done for Egypt and the world. On the tomb wall reliefs of Akhenaten's royal courtiers, depicts Akhenaten and Nefertiti- both shown larger than other figures- sitting on dual thrones as their children stand behind them as they welcomed foreign ambassadors from throughout the empire. Here, these ambassadors bring gifts from their respected homelands: chariots, gold, silver, rare animals, and so much more; even the elderly Tiye- carried on the shoulders by her servants- made the long trek for the festivities. Luckily, we have a first-hand account from one of Akhenaten's officials of the festivities:

'Appearance of the dual king Neferkheperura-sole-one-of-
 Ra and the king's great wife, Neferneferuaten-Nefertiti,
upon the great palanquin of electrum to receive the tribute
of Syria and Kush, the west and the east, every foreign land
assembled on one occasion, even the islands in the midst of
the sea, presenting tribute to the king.'

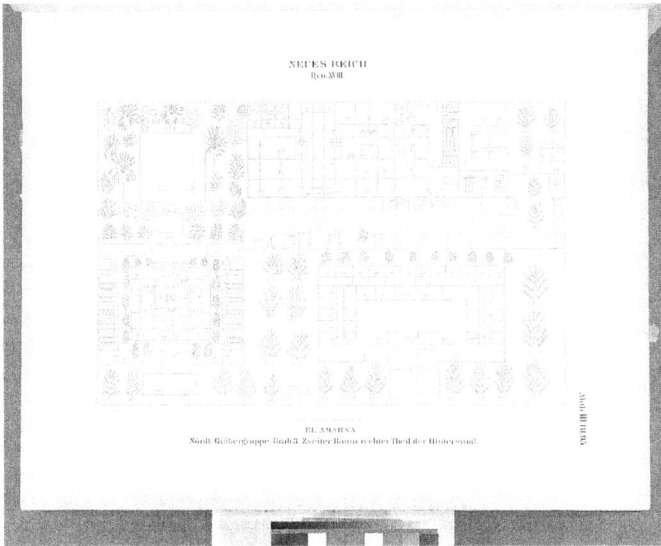

**1893 sketch of the Layout of Akhetaten.**

As Akhenaten and Nefertiti stand before the festivities, the new cult has been going on for a roughly a decade. In that short span of time, Akhenaten reestablished the pharaoh as the true dominant power in Egypt, ended priestly corruption for good, and succeeded where his father couldn't: by making the Aten, their family patron god, the one true god of all Egypt.

In his eyes, Akhenaten felt he was untouchable, and his divine power would ensure of it; however, Akhenaten was about to get a rude awakening. During that same year, Akhenaten suffered the first of many blows to come when his second daughter, Meketaten died unexpectedly. Not too long after her

**Relief of Queen Tiye (18th Dynasty)**

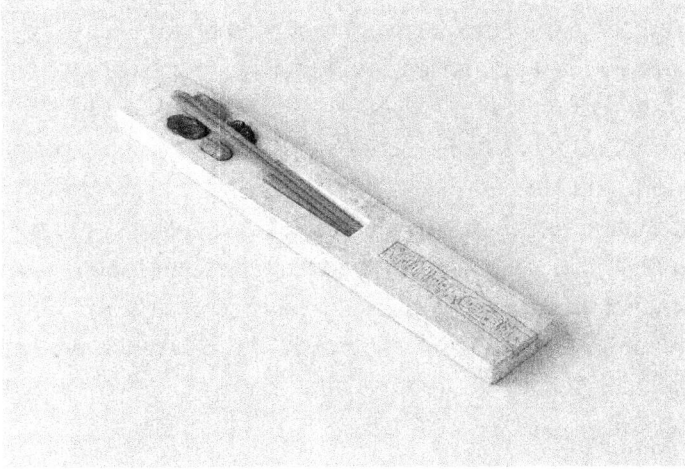

**Writing Palette with the cartouche of Meketaten (18ᵗʰ Dynasty)**

return to *Malkata,* the elderly Tiye died unexpectedly as well. The death of his mother would've devasted Akhenaten for she was the one who encouraged him in his passions but losing his daughter was just too much.

To ensure Meketaten wouldn't be alone for eternity, Akhenaten had her placed with Tiye in a tomb eight miles outside of Akhetaten The scenes coating the tomb walls depict both a grief stricken Akhenaten and Nefertiti wailing over the child. With both mother and granddaughter together, Akhenaten focused his attention on religious matters; however, what came next may have pushed Akhenaten to the brink.

# Death of the *'Great Love'*

Around the time of Meketaten and Tiye's death, Akhenaten's beloved Nefertiti vanishes from recorded history. This unexpected disappearance of Nefertiti has baffled Egyptologists and scholars alike. Why would Nefertiti suddenly disappear from recorded history? Did she lose power and simply faded? Or did she in fact die? It was the common belief that Nefertiti died in Year 12 of Akhenaten's reign due to a plague that swept across the Near East and found its way to Akhenaten's utopia. Akhenaten had received word beforehand from the King of Cyprus of the devastation this plague had on his people:

> 'the hand of Nergal is now in my country; he has slain all the men of my country. And there is not a single copper worker left.'

If true, then Nefertiti succumbed to the plague leaving Akhenaten in disarray. Nefertiti, in accordance with Akhenaten's will, be buried within the hills of Akhetaten; however, archaeologists have failed to discover any written recording of her exact death and burial.

Shortly after her death, Akhenaten elevated his remaining daughters to the position of great royal wife to ensure they would be protected if anything happens to Akhenaten. But, Akhenaten's three daughters, Setepenre, Neferneferuaten, and Tasherit, in a cruel twist of fate, disappear from recorded

**Wig inscribed with the cartouche of Nefertiti (18ᵗʰ Dynasty)**

history as well. Whether they succumbed to the plague or were purposely written out of existence, Egyptologists and archaeologists can only go by what has survived. Currently, archaeologists haven't discovered the tomb or remains of Akhenaten and Nefertiti's daughters.

## The Empire in Chaos

From the beginning of his reign, Akhenaten had been uninterested in political affairs. He believed his focus should be placed on perfecting the new Aten religion within Akhetaten and left the political issues to Nefertiti and his courtiers to deal with; however, it was due to his lack of interest, left Egypt's empire vulnerable to attack. Any military action Akhenaten faced during his reign were either too little or too late. Despite welcoming tribute from the empire, Akhenaten had failed to combat the rising crisis in the East. To compound matters, there were tensions between Akhenaten and his brothers. For instance, the Assyrian king **Asshurbalit**, wrote a scathing letter to Akhenaten over his ambassadors to stand under the open blazing sun:

'Why should [my] messengers be made to stay constantly out in the sun and die in the sun? If staying out in the sun means profit for the king, then let the messenger stay out and let him die right in the sun, but for the king himself, there must be profit. But really, why should they die in the open sun?'

It was around this time **Suppiluliumas**, King of the Hittites, spotted this weakness. By this time, the Mitanni was dealing with political in-fighting and what better way for Suppiluliumas to invade the Mitaani then by supporting the rebel army. When Tushratta wrote to Akhenaten how "blind" Akhenaten onto what's going on in the East, within his own country, and Suppiluliumas, he believed Akhenaten would change his tune, but he didn't.

Instead, Akhenaten tried forging a friendly correspondence with Suppiluliumas. Unfortunately for Tushratta, he wouldn't receive aide, from Egypt; he would be killed by Suppululiumas and the rebelling army; resulting in the Mittani to be split into

**Kingdom of Mitanni Seal 1500-1350 BC.**

two weaker kingdoms and the Hittites gaining control over the Syrian lands as far as the south Orontes River. The death of Tushratta soon became a battle cry for Egypt's imperial states to rebel against their Egyptian overlords and with one another. **Rib-Hadda**, the mayor of Byblos, desperately wrote to Akhenaten pleading for his help:

'May the king, my lord, know that the war of Abdi Ashrita against me is severe, and he has taken all my cities." After failing to hear from Akhenaten, Rib-Hadda wrote a second letter to Akhenaten, "you are going to an empty house. Everything is gone.'

Instead of receiving an answer to solve the crisis, Rib-Hadda received a scathing response from Akhenaten. "You are the one mayor that writes to me more than all the other mayors." Due to the chaos going on in the Near East, Egypt lost tribute from its imperial holdings, were denied accesses to ports, and couldn't import timber from the Mediterranean. Even Nubia took the opportunity to rebel in Year 12, but Akhenaten swiftly squashed the rebellion.

If Akhenaten acted sooner against Suppiluliumas, Egypt wouldn't have lost their imperial territories-and could continue receiving tribute-but more importantly, fractured the image of the strong warrior pharaoh.. It would take years until pharaoh **Ramses II**, for the prestige image of the pharaoh to be respected amongst the people and the Near East.

## Terror in the Streets

When Akhenaten closed off the temples in Year 5, he didn't close Egypt completely away from the gods. To please the people's anger, he allowed them to continue to worship the gods- that weren't Amun- in a reduced scale, but this act wasn't entirely equal. Those who dwelled in Akhetaten were forced to worship the Aten and the royal family; however, what Akhenaten couldn't foresee was the people secretly worshipping the gods in their own homes. Within their homes, the people of Akhetaten smuggled in small statues of protective gods and goddesses and even Amun himself.

This was an open act of defiance to Akhenaten's new philosophy and worshipping the gods in secret was a big gamble for the people to not get caught. After years of allowing his people to worship the gods, Akhenaten had enough and began to persecute Amun and the gods; by obliterating their names, and images from existence.

Across Egypt, stone masons descended onto Amun's monuments and began defacing and eradicating Amun and the gods from Egypt. In his eyes, there could be no god other than the Aten for it was the true god of all creation. Paranoid of being caught possessing or secretly worshipping any god not the Aten, caused intense fear amongst the Egyptian people. And they had every right to be afraid. Soon after, the streets were flooded with Akhenaten's soldiers forcefully

'...not only did they [pharaoh's men] set towns and villages on fire  pillaging in the temples and mutilating image of the gods without restraint but they made a practice of using the sanctuaries as kitchens to roast the sacred animals which the people worshipped; and they would compel the priests and prophets to sacrifice and butcher the beasts, afterwards casting the men forth naked.'

It got so bad, the idea of talking to one another could lead to being ousted by their neighbors for cheap rewards. For the remainder of his reign, the Egyptian people lived in constant fear of being caught by Akhenaten's thought police,

## The Reality at Akhetaten

Akhenaten believed everyone living at Akhetaten were happy knowing the evil that was Egypt's past- and priestly

**Statue's of a family living in Akhetaten (18<sup>th</sup> Dynasty)**

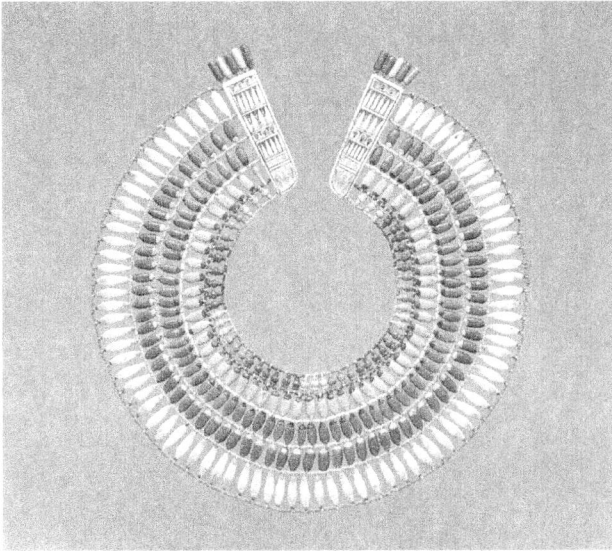

**(Top) Broad collar necklace.  (Bottom) Statuette from Akhetaten (18th Dynasty)**

**Blue storage jar from Akhetaten (18th Dynasty)**

corruption- was gone, but this couldn't be further than the truth. While the nobility was enjoying their nice cozy lives behind the great wall, the poorer citizens enjoyed a life of misery. For starters, they lived harder, if not, shorter lives. Bodies discovered in Akhetaten's desert valley tell their story: they either lacked or had no proper nutrition, spines irreparably damaged from overworking; with majority of the death rate being amongst the young.

**Wall relief sketch from Akhetaten of daily life.**

**Banquet Scene between Akhenaten and the royal family. From the tomb of Huya. Akhetaten (18ᵗʰ Dynasty)**

These people were always hungry, forbidden to steal food and drink from the *Great Aten Temple*-if caught were punished. They severely overworked and without proper nutrition, caused those to become physically stunted for the remainder of their lives. It didn't help matters that they had to endure their homes being ransacked by Akhenaten's secret tolerance police. To the people of Akhetaten, they were living under extreme authoritarianism rather than living in a utopia Akhenaten promised them. If life in the city was extreme enough for the people of Akhetaten, they had to contend with the **Medjay**. The Medjay came from Egypt's eastern deserts and were well known for one thing: as great warriors. When it came time to plan Akhetaten, Akhenaten had installed the Medjay as the city's security to not only keep the poor in check- while instilling fear- but to protect the privacy of the elite and himself.

What we know of the medjay's time at Akhetaten comes from the wall reliefs from the tomb of **Mahu** ('Chief of the Medjay of Akhetaten') in which it reveals the medjay riding across Central City in chariots, while other reliefs shows the medjay running around with blunt weapons. Those who broke the law would be hand to the medjay where they would be sent to prison camps outside Akhetaten's walls. Since these camps were out of Egypt jurisdiction, they could do whatever they wanted to the prisoners.

If prisoners escaped, they actively hunted them down and forcefully brought them back to the prison; where they were conscripted to work on building projects, in the agriculture fields, and fight in the pharaoh's army. Life both inside and outside Akhetaten proved to be more of a nightmare for the people than paradise.

## The Final Year of Akhenaten

It's hard to imagine what Akhenaten was like in his final year on the throne. An empire on the brink, the people despising him, and his family life in shambles, may have left Akhenaten broken. In Year 17, Akhenaten the radical ideological leader of the Aten dies. To this day, it's unclear if Akhenaten had lost power and faded away or died due to health complications. Whatever the case may be, Akhenaten was buried in his tomb on the Eastern cliffs of Akhetaten- his body was placed in a pink granite sarcophagus and was accompanied with magic

**Akhenaten, Nefertiti, and the Aten illustration.**

bricks, canopic jars, shabti, and four statues of his beloved Nefertiti to watch over him. Even in death, Nefertiti had power as she did in life and would watch over Akhenaten. With the absence of Akhenaten, any power the Aten once had died alongside with him. As the opening to the tomb was sealed, Akhenaten would be left alone to overlook his grand utopia as the Aten life-giving rays continue to bless and rejuvenate his tomb till the end of time.

# 12

# Undoing The Damage

After the death of Akhenaten in 1336 BC, Egypt was plunged into political turmoil. In the wake of his death, Akhenaten's loyal acolytes wished to continue their pharaoh's revolution that was "working" for Egypt; however, they face opposition from an old friend: the Amun priesthood. When Ipetsut was forced closed by Akhenaten in Year 5, the Amun priesthood had been patiently biding their time- until Akhenaten had either slipped up or died- and seized the opportunity to restore traditional orthodoxy to Egypt. With two rival factions fighting for Egypt's future, the royal family were at a crossroads: do they continue to enforce Akhenaten's ideology and face alienation from the people or side with the Amun priesthood and restore religious orthodoxy to the country?

These questions plagued the new leader of the country a man named **Ankhkperurue Smenkhkare**, but who was this mysterious man? During the tail end of his reign (1339 BC), Akhenaten had named Ankhkperurue Smenkhkare his co-

Regent, yet the life of this man has been shrouded in mystery. For the longest time, Egyptologists had been trying to put the pieces together of Ankhkperurue Smenkhkare's relation to Akhenaten. There are those who believe he was another son of Akhenaten had with Kiya or a royal acolyte Akhenaten strongly favored or was the husband of Meretaten-which gave him more leeway to the throne than those in court.

However, these theories fall apart due to lack of archaeological evidence. Recently, it has come to light that Ankhkperurue Smenkhkare wasn't an acolyte, a son, or in-law, but was in fact Nefertiti herself. How could this be? Egyptologists had noticed Ankhkperurue Smenkhkare had a secondary name Ankhkperurue Neferneferuaten. The latter name intrigued Egyptologists and propose Nefertiti was Smenkhkare.

Moret recently, a discovery was made at the quarry site of **Dayr Abu Hinnis** and it was here where archaeologists discovered an inscription. '*Great King's Wife, his beloved mistress of the Two Lands, Neferneferuaten Nefertiti.*' At first, archaeologists thought it was written sometime before her death, only to be shocked to discover it was written in Year 16; one year before Akhenaten's death. If true, then Nefertiti didn't succumb to the plague as previously thought and lived long enough to take power for herself.

It would make sense if this was Nefertiti since she was named Akhenaten's co-regent, knew the ins and outs of the government, mastered every ritual for the Aten, and was trusted by Akhenaten to continue his philosophy, but therein lies the issue with Nefertiti being Ankhkperurue Neferneferuaten: the name.

**Mold containing the cartouche of Smenkhkare (18ᵗʰ Dynasty)**

The new discovery generated new theories amongst Egyptologists that Ankhkperurue Smenkhkare is the masculine name- and the third name change- to Nefertiti's feminine Ankhkperurue Nefernferuaten. Egyptologists speculate the marriage between Smenkhkare and Meretaten was a symbolic gesture to fulfill rituals to the Aten. Although this new discovery changes our view of thelatter Amarna Period, there Egyptologists who fiercely disagree Nefertiti wasn't Smenkhkare, but whatever the case maybe, what did

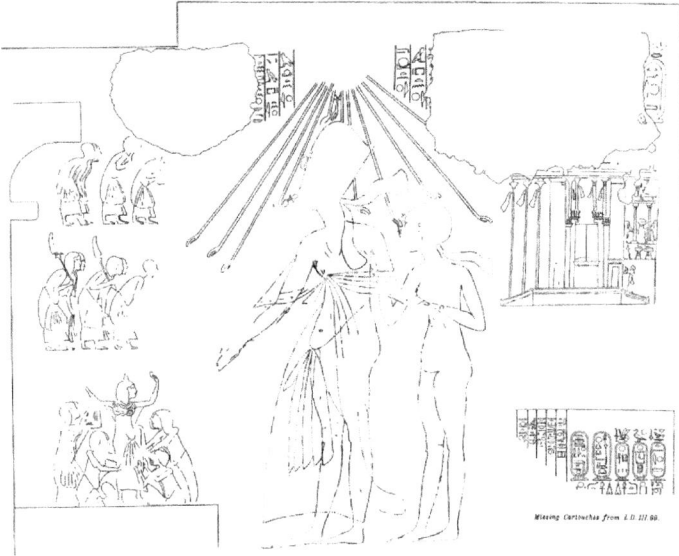

**Wall relief of Smenkhkare/Nefertiti and Meretaten (18th Dynasty)**

Ankhkperurue Smenkhkare/Nefertiti accomplish in her short tenure as pharaoh?

## The Short Reign of Ankhkperurue Smenkhkare's

If Ankhkperurue Smenkhkare was Nefertiti, what lay ahead was an uneasy task to heal the wounds Akhenaten had inflicted onto the people. One of her first tasks was to gradually abandon Akhetaten as a sign of not only peace but as a token of apologizing for Akhenaten's wrongdoing; trying to gain back the people's trust. Ankhkperurue Smenkhkare next step was to slowly reestablish the Amun priesthood to society. This may look like Ankhkperurue Smenkhare/Nefertiti was betraying Akhenaten's ideology; however, the cult of the Aten was still in power. Smenkhkare even went as far as reopening some of the temples across Egypt not for religious purposes, but for monetary means. By the end of Akhenaten's reign, Egypt was bankrupt. Akhenaten had spent ludicrous amounts of Egypt's wealth on Sed Festivals, expanding his new cult and the construction of Akhetaten itself. But how could Egypt be bankrupt if they had tribute and gold from Nubia?

Majority of Egypt's wealth was taken from the Amun priesthood, taxes, and tribute, but due to the closing of the temples, the turmoil going on in the Near East, and Akhenaten's overspending, resulted in a fractured country. Ankhkperurue Smenkhkare/Nefertiti's reign would come to an end in 1333 BC, when she disappears from records. As of now, archaeologists haven't found any physical evidence of Ankhkperurue Smenkhkare; however, her early actions at restoration were the first to heal the country.

## Crowning of the Boy King

During the reign of Ankhkperurue Smenkhkare/Nefertiti short time on the throne, discontent within the royal court began to grow. There were loyalists who sided with Akhenaten's decision naming Ankhkperurue Smenkhkare/ Nefertiti as his co-regent and as the rightful ruler, while traditionalists insisted Smenkhkare was taking away true power from the rightful king: Akhenaten's son, Tutankhaten. For nearly a century, it has been speculated if Tutankhaten truly was the son of Akhenaten; however, an inscription from Hermpolis confirms

Head sculpt of Tutankhaten. Located today at the Berlin
Museum (18th Dynasty)

that indeed Tutankhaten was the son of Akhenaten. "the king's bodily son, his beloved, Tutakhaten." The traditionlists believed the now nine-year-old Tutankhaten was the true heir to Akhenaten, but why did they wait till now to make Tutankhaten the next pharaoh?

Within this faction, reactionary forces wanted a leader who would follow their ideology, their views and was easy to manipulate. There is also the question as to why Akhenaten didn't name Tutankhaten his successor first; however it can be speculated Akhenaten had more trust in Nefertiti to carry on his philosophy. He may have wanted to keep Tutankhaten out of the spotlight- so outside forces wouldn't instigate their policies over and eradicate his owns. After conversing with the high priest of Amun, the royal court and military general **Horemheb** unanimously agreed Tutankhaten was the rightful heir.

Their first action was to convince the royal court for Tutankhaten to be crowned in Memphis to show the people their new pharaoh was for Egypt's traditions and not Akhenaten's heretical ideals. In 1334 BC, the nine-year old Tutankhaten was crowned pharaoh; however, he needed a queen. To strengthen his legitimacy to the throne, the royal court convinced Tutankhaten to marry his half-sister Ankhesenpaaten- who by this time had gained the title of great wife.

Despite being a child, Tutankhaten still needed supervision and a teacher to guide him. To rectify this issue, the royal court had Tutankhaten's inherited vizier and uncle, Ay to be his guide in these uncertain times- though secretly had his own political ambitions.

**Lepsius sketch of a wall relief of Tutankhamun.**

## Return to Normalcy

Now as pharaoh, Tutankhaten had to begin the arduous process to restore normalcy to the country. In Tutankhaten's first year, he returned the royal court-stationed at Akhetaten- back to Memphis. To show his sympathy to the people and not his father's views, Tutankhaten renounced his birth name by changing it to **Tutankhamun** ('*The Living Image of Aten*') and had his queen change her name from Ankesenpaaten to **Ankhesenamun** ('*She Lives for Amun*'). Now as the newly rechristened Tutankhamun, Tutankhamun restored Amun as Egypt's prominent god and denounced the Aten; ordering the royal family to abandon the city for good and return to Thebes. To commemorate his break from Akheaten's Atenist ideology, Tutankhamun issued a new plan known as the **Great Restoration Decree**:

'When His Majesty became king, the temples of the gods and goddesses from Abu to the delta marshes…had fallen into ruin. Their shrines had fallen into decay, having become mounds thick with weeds….The land was in distress; the gods had abandoned this land. If armies were sent to the Near East to widen the borders of Egypt, they had no success. If one made supplications to a god for protection, he did not come at all.'

According to his speech Tutankhamun was declaring to the people- and by extent Egypt- how Akhenaten's heresy forced the gods to abandon Egypt and its people to perpetual chaos and promised he would restore the gods back to prominence; by fully reopening the closed temples, restore the priesthoods back to relevancy, and create new cult status as a token to this new promise.

Once proposing his promise to the people, Tutankhamun went to work by ordering damages done to the cult's temples and Amun's temple by Akhenaten's cronies to be restored. In

Golden chair depicting Tutankhamun and Ankhesenamun.
18th Dynasty

**Head sculpt of Tutankhamun. 18<sup>th</sup> Dynasty**

Memphis, Tutankhamun had created a new temple called '*the house of Nebkheperura*' that restored Ptah and his traditional ceremonies to the people. To show his gratitude to Amun, Tutankhamun gave the priesthood a hefty compensation as a token of apology for Akhenaten's actions. While in Thebes, Tutankhamun ordered new temple complexes to be constructed in the name of Amun and it's here within the new temples lies an inscription from a large stele going over Tutankhamun's hopes for a return to normalcy:

'When his Person appeared as king, the temples and cities of gods and goddesses, starting from Elephantine as far as the Delta marshes…were fallen into decay and their shrines were fallen into ruin, having become mere mounds overgrown with grass. Their sanctuaries were like something which had not yet come into being and their buildings were a footpath for the land was in rack and ruin. The gods were ignoring this land…if one prayed to a god, to ask something from him, he did not come at all; and if one beseeched any goddess in the same way, she did not come at all….'

For a time, it appeared Egypt was finally returning to normalcy; however, Tutankhamun wasn't quite done. One action he took personally was appointing new priests he trusted would not go rogue and rebel against him; issuing an overseer to keep the priesthood in check and to make sure the temples were both properly funded and equipped with whatever they needed to make offerings to the gods.

Tutankhamun even went as far as forbidding the relaxed realism of Amarna art style and returned the emotionless, youthful, and divine depictions back into Egyptian art. In terms of foreign affairs, Tutankhamun ordered Horemheb to combat Suppilulimas and restore Egypt's imperial territories- while restoring the image of the pharaoh as the warrior pharaoh. Yes, it would seem Egypt was slowly returning to the glory days of Amenhotep III, but tragedy was soon to follow.

## Death of the Boy King

Just as he was reaching to adulthood, tragedy struck when Tutankhamun unexpectedly died in 1323 BC. He was around eighteen or nineteen when he died. In the wake of his death, Egypt fell into a new crisis: Tutankhamun had died with no male heir to succeed him. Throughout their decade long marriage, Tutankhamun and Ankesnamun had two daughters, yet both tragically died in childbirth. Their two children would be mummified and buried with Tutankhamun.

On the outset of his death, Ay seized his chance to gain power. It's been theorized if all these reforms and restorations weren't done by Tutankhamun at all but was in fact enacted by Ay himself- who disguised his deeds using Tutankhamun's name. To seize power for himself, Ay married his own granddaughter, the now widowed Ankhensanamun. Fear of the marriage, Ankhensanamun secretly wrote to Suppiluliumas himself to send one of his sons for her to marry.

This act could be read as a Ankhensanamun betraying Egypt by giving the enemy a foothold in the country, or possibly a friendly alliance with the Hittites, but this was not meant to be. After months of stalling, Suppilulimas sent one of his sons to

**(Top) Opening of the Mouth Ceremony. (Bottom) Tutankhamun embracing Osiris (18th Dynasty)**

**Amun-Ra (seated) presenting Tutankhamun (missing head and right arm) as his suitable heir. Notice there is no sign of the Aten showing how dedicated the Egyptians were to eliminate any trace of the Aten's visage in art- even if the Aten's name was presented in cartouches (18<sup>th</sup> Dynasty)**

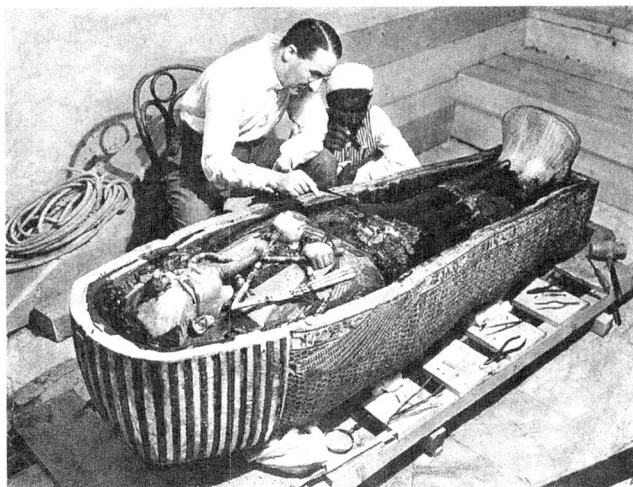

**(Top/Bottom) Archaeologist Howard Carter examining the open sarcophagus of Tutankhamun.**

**Tutankhamun's Golden Death Mask (18ᵗʰ Dynasty)**

marry Ankhensanamun; however, this secret was found out by Ay's spies. As the young Hittite prince was traveling through Palestine, he was taken by surprise by a small group of Egyptian soldiers and was brutally murdered.

After the death of the Hittite prince, Ankhensamun vanishes from history. To this day, archaeologists have not found the tomb or mummy of Ankhenseamun. Ay's time on the throne would be brief- by the time he came to power he was an elderly man- and after four years on the throne dies

## Erasing Akhenaten

By the time Tutankhamun succeed Akhenaten in 1332 BC, Horemheb had come to prominence as commander in chief of the Egyptian army. He was given immense titles that illustrated his newfound powers: '*King's Two Eyes Throughout the Two Banks, King's Deputy in Every Place, Foremost of the King's Courtiers, Overseer of Generals of the Lord of the Two Lands, Overseer of Every Office of the King, Overseer of Overseers of the Two Banks, Overseer of All Divine Offices, Hereditary Prince of Upper and Lower Egypt*'. He was given the task as the young boy king's protector. Horemheb flexed his influence over the direction of government policy, and from his office at Memphis, he must have been one of the chief architects of the return to normalcy, not Tutankhamun.

The last title seems to make Horemheb Tutankhamun's true heir. It appears Horemheb was closely involved in every department of government, and it may be suspected that was the effective power in the land, the de facto ruler in a country where the king was still a minor.

**Wall relief of Ay and his wife Tey. 18ᵗʰ Dynasty**

Despite such a raft of responsibilities, Horemheb did not turn his back on his main profession and powerbase: the army. The walls in his private tomb at Saqqara- built during the reign of Tutankhamun- were decorated with scenes of his military career. At the time of Tutankhamun's death, Horemheb was away leading an unsuccessful campaign in Syria-to recapture

**Stilua with the cartouche containing Akhenaten's name is erased. 18th Dynasty**

the rebellious city of Kadesh from the Hittites- when he heard about Tutankhamun's untimely death and missed his opportunity to becoming pharaoh and now had to bide his time, luckily for Horemheb, he didn't have to wait too long. Horemheb knew Ay's time was coming to an end and after four years of waiting, and the backing of the military,

Horemheb seized his chance for the throne. He proclaimed he was Tutankhamun's true heir and was merely fulfilling his destiny. One of Horemheb's first action as pharaoh was to legitimize his claim to the throne.

He did this by "airbrushing" the intervening reigns from history, so that he could present himself as the first rightful pharaoh since Egypt's "dazzling orb." He did this by re-carving all of Tutankhamun's inscriptions and monuments with his own names and titles, so that he could take the sole credit for the return to orthodoxy- in which he claims he was the true puppet master while Tutankhamun was the puppet.

To this end, Horemheb ordered Akhenaten's temples at *Gempaaten* to be systematically dismantled, their blocks used as fill for his own constructions. On his orders, teams of workmen descended upon Akhetaten and began expunging not only all traces of Akhenaten, but all statues of Akhenaten and Nefertiti were torn down, smashed, and tossed into a heap outside *The Great Aten Temple*. In a final insult, Horemheb cursed Akhenaten as '*that criminal of Akhetaten*' and forbid his name to never be utter again. Unbeknownst to Horemheb, he indirectly preserved Akhenaten's memory.

# 13

# Why Akhenaten's Plan Failed

Over the course of his tumultuous reign, Akhenaten had eliminated centuries of tradition in favor to promote his personal god, the Aten. In his eyes, Akhenaten believed his new philosophy of the Aten would continue for eons; however, this monotheistic religion was destined to fail. How could this be? While it's agreed upon Egyptologists that Akhenaten's revolution was politically driven to strip the Amun priesthood of political power, it was also seen as a grand experiment. For starters, Egypt's polytheistic pantheon of gods were inclusive to everyday life for the Egyptians because they believed the gods were not only amongst them but were living side by side with their creations.

In terms of the monotheistic cult of the Aten, it was entirely exclusive as Akhenaten excluded the gods from everyday life. A great example was Akhetaten itself. Those who were forced to live in Akhetaten were forced to worship Akhenaten and his family as the new gods-dwelling amongst "their" creation serving as the creator of the universe- and everyone had to accept it no questions asked. But the most damaging thing

**Head sculpt of Amun-Ra. 18ᵗʰ Dynasty**

Akhenaten inflicted onto his own people was denying a suitable afterlife.

## Denying the Afterlife

The Egyptians believed their whole existence was to prepare for the greatness of the afterlife. Due to the concept of duality, the Egyptians knew their next life would be just like how they lived life but only better because the gods had made it beautiful. Therefore, every ritual had to be performed perfectly in life, the moment of death, and even after death- the mummification process, the Opening of the Mouth Ceremony

The Egyptian trinity: Hours (left) Osiris (middle), and Isis (right)

Blue turquoise shabti of Akhenaten. 18<sup>th</sup> Dynasty

**Weighing of the Heart Ceremony**

that allowed the deceased body to use its ears, mouth, eyes, ears, nose for the next life - to ensure the **Ka** (the lifeforce given the moment at birth) and the **Ba** (the physical body represented by a human head on a bird) could come together be able travel to the underworld; however, the journey to the next life was wrought with danger.

The moment the deceased begins its journey, they had to endure untold nightmares ranging from fighting off demons to being devoured by them, but if their mummified body was given protective charms, they would be protected from these creatures. Once the deceased endured the long arduous journey, they would be welcomed by the god Anubis; from there, he would personally escort the deceased to the Hall of Judgment.

Within the hall laid a grand jury of forty-two gods and at the end of the court laid Osiris overseeing the final judgment of the deceased. At its center, was a large balance (scale) where the next phase the deceased must pass: weighing of the heart. Before his/her heart was placed, they had to make a "confession"-to every judge and Osiris-that they didn't commit any crime in their life and lived accordingly with the will of Maat. From there, their, the heart was taken from the deceased and was placed on the scale against the ostrich feather of Maat.

If the scale was perfectly balanced, then the deceased was allowed access to the next world where the Ka and Ba united together. Through this rebirth, the soul becomes the **Akh** (the living soul) but if the heart weighed more than the feather, the heart was given to Ammut, the Gobbler of Shadows- a creature with the head of an alligator, the body of a lion, and the legs of a hippopotamus-. The Ammut would be given the tainted heart to feast on. Once eaten, the deceased seize to exist. Unfortunately, this inclusive promise of a better life after death became exclusive to the people by Akhenaten's philosophy.

## Akhenaten's Afterlife

During his reign, Akhenaten had himself and Nefertiti depicted wearing a special crown called the Atef crown. The Atef crown, coated with large ostrich feathers (the symbols of Shu) bull horns and adorned with the Aten (in the guise as the sun disc), was originally worn by Osiris himself. To have himself and Nefertiti depicted with the Atef crown meant Akhenaten was the god Osiris and had the power over life and death.

In his new ideology, Akhenaten proclaimed the Aten had the ability to continually renew itself-undergoing its entire lifespan from dawn to dusk, only to undergo its own rebirth- daily. Due to this power, life in the universe would undergo its own rebirth. In this radical view, Akhenaten proclaimed there was no life after death, only a promise to live forever under the Aten's life-giving rays but the promise of an afterlife was only given to Akhenaten and his family.

For starters, those who died during Akhenaten's reign were closed off from the afterlife. Consequently, the deceased were chained to the mortal world as wondering ghosts, who by day, haunted the Aten's altars and Akhetaten, and at night were forced to return to their tombs. They would repeat this process over and over for eternity-as Akhenaten and the royal family dodged this fate.

Since they were the children of the Aten, Akhenaten and the royal family enjoyed not only a joyous afterlife but an eternal life amongst the Aten. This is what ultimately doomed the revolution: Akhenaten failed to give his people any hope for a better afterlife. To the people living in these hectic times, they believed their pharaoh allowed chaos to reign free which caused every bad instance to happen to Egypt-driving Egypt to go bankrupt, losing their imperial territories in the Near East; while destroying the image of the pharaoh. Which is why the people of Egypt had to erase Akhenaten to correct the mistake thrusted onto them unjustly, return to normalcy, and reestablish balance in the universe. If Akhenaten had promised a better afterlife for everyone- and not himself or family- it

**Funerary figure of Akhenaten (18ᵗʰ Dynasty)**

Broken piece of Akhenaten's mouth and nose (18<sup>th</sup> Dynasty)

then the citizens may have been swayed to worshipping the Aten as the main god, but still would have rejected Akhenaten's heresy.

Ultimately, Egypt had failed to stop Akhenaten's tyrannical rule. With an overflowing income of gold and trade goods, made the people complacent to go along with everything; resulting in Akhenaten's power grab of the country. The priests, with all their wealth, could have taken the throne away from Akhenaten; however, it was their greed that doomed Egypt. After his death, the Egyptian people made sure to erase Akhenaten, but defacing his images, destroying his monuments and statues, would not have gotten rid of him entirely; it only preserved his legacy as history's first monotheistic ruler in recorded history.

# 14

# Akhenaten Found?

It was a cool afternoon on January 6, 1907, when American archaeologist **Theodore M. Davis** was overseeing his latest excavation in the Valley of The Kings. Theodore Davis was a wealthy financier from Newport, Rhode Island who would spend his winter holidays in Egypt. It was during his stay on his Egyptian '*dahabiya*' (traditional Egyptian boat) where Davis became interested in Egyptology. With his vast wealth, Davis was able to finance any excavations in Egypt for any price, yet he focused his attention on the Valley of The Kings.

A few years prior, Davis had struck gold when he discovered the tomb of Tiye's parents Yuya and Thuya. Davis had hope, this season in the Valley would not only yield an even bigger discovery but solidify his name in the annals of history as the greatest archaeologist. As he sat in the shade sipping his coffee, thinking of what new riches he would find, Davis was suddenly alerted by his excavator that they found something.

 In his excitement, Davis rushed over to where his excavator, named **Edward Ayrton**, had made the discovery. Apparently, Ayrton, digging near the tomb of Rameses XI, had unknowingly struck a limestone wall revealing a flight of stairs: the telltale signs of a royal tomb. To put this in context, before King Tutankhamun's discovery in 1922, tombs discovered in the Valley were usually ransacked, missing their mummies, broken pottery scattered throughout, stripped of their treasures, and even the wall reliefs.

Despite these tombs not being entirely intact, their richly decorated tombs have given Egyptologists and scholars a better understanding of Egyptian civilization. With the prospect of an intact royal tomb, just a few feet from him, Davis and Ayrton descended into the tomb. As they made their way through the tomb, Davis and Ayrton noticed oddities within the tomb itself. First, the tomb had a sloping corridor which led them to a cramped square chamber. Ayrton would later recount his take of their descent down into the tomb:

"…we made a thorough clearance down to the entrance of the tomb which had evidently been begun on a smaller scale then enlarged. We found the doorway closed by a loosely-built wall of limestone fragments resting not on the rock beneath but on the loose rubbish which had filled the stairway. This we removed and found behind it the remains of the original sealing of the door…on this we found the impressions of the oval seal of the priestly college of Amun-Ra at Thebes-a jackal crouching over nine captives…"

It appeared Ayrton and Davis stumbled upon an intact sealed tomb, with both men's hearts racing at the prospect of treasure waiting behind the limestone wall. After removing the wall of the tomb, Davis and Ayrton discovered this tomb contained a single squared chamber.

The squared chamber was in total disarray: undecorated walls, building debris scattered across the condensed chamber, vast pieces of what was once funerary items, and tools lazily left behind from workers. A few meters ahead, Ayrton had noticed what appeared to be the remains of what appeared to be a dismantled wooden shrine covered in gold leaf.

According to the hieroglyphic texts on the wooden shrine, this shrine belonged to none other than Queen Tiye. At the tomb's southern walls, Davis and Ayrton found four alabaster jar stoppers (near the right wall of the tomb) with female heads sporting the Nubian-style wigs worn by Akhenaten's daughters and Nefertiti during the Amarna period. However, at the southern wall of the tomb, laid a decayed wooden sarcophagus. The sarcophagus, according to Egyptologists, "represents perhaps the most controversial archaeological discovery made in Egypt".

## The Sarcophagus Controversy

The tomb, known today as *KV55*, Davis, and Ayrton discovered back in 1907, would become of Egypt's most controversial discoveries. When Davis and Ayrton first discovered the sarcophagus, it was in terrible condition; with the once beautiful golden leaf face adorning the sarcophagus was brutally torn off (leaving behind only it's right eye and eyebrow). However, what caught the eye of Davis and Ayrton, was the missing cartouche on the lid of the sarcophagus. At some point, the cartouche once held the name of the individual

**Edward Russell Ayrton**

but at some point, was hacked out. Why would the Egyptians go out of their way to remove the name of this individual?

Whoever this individual was, had to be important since only the pharaoh and the royal family could be buried in the Valley of the Kings. To solve this mystery, both Davis and Ayrton decided to open the sarcophagus to see if there was an intact mummy or not. Luckily for them, there was an intact mummy, but according to Ayrton, the mummy was not in the best condition:

"….presently we cleared the mummy from the coffin and found that that smallish person, with a delicate head and hands….I gently touched one of the front teeth (3,000 years old) and alas! it fell into dust, thereby showing that the mummy could not be preserved. We then took off the gold crown, and attempted to remove the mummy cloth in which the body was wrapped, but the moment I attempted to lift a bit of the wrapping it came off in a black mass, exposing the ribs…."

What Davis and Ayrton found in the sarcophagus was the remains of the damaged mummy. The sarcophagus and the mummy had the misfortune of being placed right underneath a crack on the surface of the tomb-where water had been slowly dripping onto the sarcophagus for centuries.

Around the mummy's head was an elegant gold vulture that may have been used as a pectoral or collar decoration. It's believed this mummy had a golden death mask covering its

The damaged sarcophagus of KV55. Notice the golden leaf removed from the headdress, the face nearly ripped off, and the cartouche etched out in the center (18th Dynasty)

**The destroyed face of the KV 55 Sarcophagus (18ᵗʰ Dynasty)**

head and was probably stolen later, but why the robbers decide to leave the mummy with its golden collar is still unknown. Davis, after careful observations of the tomb, concluded this mummy had to belong to Queen Tiye.

He argued since the wooden shrine bore Tiye's name and the four alabaster stoppers not only fall in line with the style of the Amarna period but were, in fact, meant this had to be Tiye's tomb. If this was Tiye's tomb, then why was her name hacked out from "her" sarcophagus? And more importantly, if Davis' assumptions are correct, then why are there '*magic bricks*' containing Akhenaten's name?

## Is the Mummy Male or Female?

Theodore Davis believed the mummy found in KV55 belonged to Tiye, but due to the poor condition of the mummified remains, he wasn't entirely sure if the mummy was either male or female. The mummy, after centuries of water damage, was left with only its bones intact. To prove his theory, Davis enlisted the help of American physician **Dr. Pollock**, who happened to be vacationing in Egypt that year. After careful examination of the mummy, Pollock confirmed Davis' theory about the mummy in KV55 was, in fact, a woman. When asked by Chief Inspector of Antiquities **Arthur Weigall** about the validity of the mummy's gender, Pollock's answer was completely different. "I saw Dr. Pollock in Luxor the other day, who denies that he ever thought that it was a woman, and he says the other doctor could not be sure".

After Pollock's examinations, other physicians began examining the mummy, and all came to the same conclusion of the remains belonging to a woman. With his theory proven correct, Davis went on ahead with his claim of KV55 belonging to Queen Tiye, with his 1910 book called The Tomb of Queen Tiyi.

Two years after Davis published his findings, an anatomist named **Grafton Elliot Smith**, decided he would conduct his own examination of the mummy. In his examination of the mummy, Smith "empathically announced that the skeleton was male [and] [e]very expert who has since examined the bones has agreed with this reassessment." Many Egyptologists were

**Head stopper of Kiya with the distinct headdress from the Amarna Period. From the tomb of KV55 (18th Dynasty)**

**Full canopic jar of Kiya. From the tomb of KV55 (18th Dynasty)**

**Arthur Weigall standing next to a giant statue of Horus.**

already skeptical of Davis' claim of the tomb belonging to Tiye, however, they do agree with Smith's examination of the mummy being male, but there was a problem. Who did the bones of this individual belong to?

While Egyptologists were struggling in identifying the nameless male mummy of KV55, Arthur Weigall proposed his own theory of the identity of the mummy: Akhenaten. Weigall deduced the tomb and the mummy had to belong to Akhenaten due to his name inscribed on 'magic bricks' found in the tomb:

In view of their cheap nature and ready manufacture, it is exceedingly improbable one king's brick would have been utilized for the burial of another or would have been regarded as effective for that purpose without a change of name. we have no option, therefore, but to conclude that [KV 55] served as the burial chamber of Akhenaten and his was the body within the coffin."

Weigall noted Akhenaten's name was inscribed on thin gold ribbons discovered on the mummy. These ribbons would later be stolen after KV55's discovery. If the mummy belongs to Akhenaten, then why was his mummy placed in a sarcophagus originally made for a woman? Egyptologists began speculating who was the original owner of the sarcophagus and noted at one point the sarcophagus was made for a woman.

The texts on the sarcophagus contained feminine endings that were meant for a royal female (with noticeable signs of a false beard and the uraeus). Some argued the sarcophagus was made for Tutankhamun's mother Kiya due to several seals containing the boy king's name. This has led Egyptologists to conclude this scenario: at some point, Akhenaten, Kiya, and even Queen Tiye was taken from their original tombs at Akhetaten and placed in KV55.

This was possibly under Tutankhamun's orders so he can be closer to his family. Egyptologists went as far as stating the mummy could, in fact, be the mysterious and infamous Smenkhkare/Nefertiti, but many agreed the mummy had to be Akhenaten.

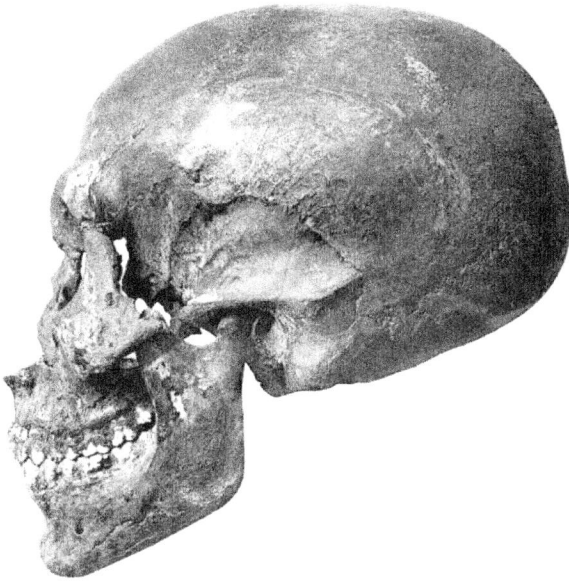

**The skull of the KV 55 mummy. Does the skull belong
to Akhenaten or Smenkhkare/Nefertiti?**

## How old is the Mummy?

It would appear, after examining the confines of the tomb, the
mummy of KV55 was the final resting place for Akhenaten,
yet the confusion as to why physicians believed the mummy
was female may have to do with the bone structure and age. At
first glance, the remains had what appeared to be woman sized
hips. The only pharaoh to be portrayed with the feminine hips
was Akhenaten, but when Smith examined the mummy back in

1912, he deduced the skeleton's age to be around twenty-five when he died.

During the 1920s, another examination of the mummy was conducted this time by **Dr. Douglas Derry** who came to a similar age of the mummy being between twenty-twenty five years old. Then, in 1963, **Professor Ronald Harrison** (from Liverpool University) conducted his own examination and concluded the mummy was around twenty-five years old. The mummy of KV55 would go on to have further examinations and after every examination, the examiners came to the same conclusion: the mummy had died in his early to mid-twenties.

The conclusions conducted on the mummy of KV55 proved to be more problematic with the prevailing theory the mummy being Akhenaten. Most Egyptologists agreed Akhenaten had died when he was around thirty-five to forty years old. This would mean Akhenaten became pharaoh when he was either eighteen or his early twenties, but according to all the examinations, the mummy was twenty-five when he died, thus couldn't be Akhenaten.

If Akhenaten did die in his twenties, then that would mean Akhenaten became Amenhotep III's co-regent when he was around six years old which contradicts the evidence of Akhenaten having full-grown children. Egyptologists began shifting their focus on the possibility the mummy was now the mysterious Smenkhkare/Nefertiti.

A recent examination of the remains, conducted by a specialized team headed by Egypt's Supreme Council of Antiquities, came up with their own estimation of the mummy's age now to be around thirty-five to forty-five years

The mummy of Tutankhamun.
Taken in the late 1920's

old. This new age would lead credence for the mummy to be Akhenaten, but due to the mummy's poor state, it is hard to determine the true age of the individual.

## New Evidence

In 2008, **Dr. Zahi Hawass**, then Head of the Supreme Council of Antiquities, led a new expedition to uncover the mystery of Tutankhamun's family lineage by analyzing the boy king's DNA to ten mummies. Hawass suspected these ten mummies could be related to Tutankhamun. "In the past, I had been against genetic studies of royal mummies," Hawass wrote to National Geographic. "

The chance of obtaining workable samples while avoiding contamination from modern DNA seemed too small to justify disturbing these sacred remains." After being convinced by highly respected geneticists, did Hawass allow the geneticists to abstract DNA from the mummies. Hawass had two state-of-the-art DNA sequencing labs commissioned. One in the basement of the Cairo Museum, led by Egyptian scientists **Yehia Gad** and **Somaia Ismail**. They were responsible for gathering information on the mummy's descriptions, backstories, and the mummies themselves.

Another team, led by **Ashraf Selim** and **Sahar Saleem**, was to conduct CT scans of the mummies at Cairo University's Faculty of Medicine. Together, these two teams would unveil the possible identities of Tutankhamun's royal family and possibly the revelation of the unnamed mummy of KV55. To extract DNA from the mummies' remains, geneticists had to remove deep tissue samples to determine if their DNA was pure. These tissue samples were extracted within the mummy's bones, but for Hawass, he was concerned the DNA was contaminated. During the mummification processes, the embalmers would pour a large amount of resin into the sarcophagus which resulted in the body sticking to the sarcophagus (which could corrode the DNA over the centuries).

Hawass was also concerned the DNA was contaminated by past archaeologists who would use their bare hands (no gloves) when dissecting mummified bodies, but what made Hawass anxious the most was the mummy's safety. By 2008, these ten mummies were in terrible condition. If the geneticists made one tiny mistake, the mummy could fall apart.

Once the geneticists safely extracted the DNA from all ten mummies, they went to work on purifying their DNA of foreign substances. Hawass grew weary of the purification process for each mummies' DNA since each mummy was embalmed differently. Each geneticist had to take different steps when extracting the foreign substances from the DNA. Despite his fears, the geneticists were able to safely secure DNA samples from the mummies of Amenhotep III, Yuya, and the mysterious mummy of KV55.

To determine the connection the mummy of KV55's DNA had with the royal family, geneticists decided to compare the mummy's *Y chromosome* with Amenhotep III's and Tutankhamun. The Y chromosome, inherited from the father, The Y chromosome, inherited from the father, was the determining factor to the mummy of KV55's relationship to the royal family, yet the Y chromosome wasn't enough.

**Colossi head of Amenhotep III**

Geneticists used the *genome patterns* (the *A's, G's, T's, C's,* that makes up our genetic code) of all three candidates. If the mummy of KV55's genetic code lined up with Amenhotep III's or Tutankhamun's, in a sequence of similar letters with the letters repeating ten times, then he was related, but if the pattern repeated twenty times with no similar letters, then he wasn't related.

After thorough examinations of the mummy of KV55's genetic code, the geneticists had made a shocking discovery. According to their findings, the lettered sequence the mummy of KV55 shared not only an exact match to Amenhotep III but with Tutankhamun's as well. This would make the mummy of KV 55 the son of Amenhotep III and the father of the boy king.

## Is the KV55 Mummy Akhenaten?

With conclusive evidence the mummy of KV55 being related to both Amenhotep III and Tutankhamun, it would stand to reason then the identity of the mummy would be none other than the heretic pharaoh Akhenaten. However, this wouldn't be the case. Even Hawass was skeptical if the mummy was either Akhenaten or Smenkhkare/Nefertiti and instead leaned towards the age of the mummy's body when he died. It's still believed by Egyptologists the mummy found in KV55 was around twenty-five years old when he died, making him too young to be Akhenaten.

Another clue to the identity of the mummy of KV55 stems from his association with Tutankhamun. The geneticists discovered both Tutankhamun and the mummy of KV55 shared the same blood type and elongated skulls called platycephalic (flat-topped or broad shaped head).

Recently, **Dr. Jamie Harris** studied the skulls of Tutankhamun and the KV55 mummy and "suggested that Tutankhamun and the KV55 body were first-degree relatives, either a father and son or full brothers." As science continues to expand and evolve, we can only hope the day would come when we will get the definitive truth of the mummy of KV55 being Akhenaten.

Unless there is another examination on the body of KV55 or a discovery of a new tomb, Egyptologists are claiming the identity of the mummy of KV55 being Akhenaten himself. At long last, the once forgotten and heretical pharaoh of Egypt is finally home. Today, Akhenaten's body resides at the Cairo Museum for all the world to see and is still regarded as one of Egypt's mysterious pharaohs of all time.

# Bibliography

Clayton, A. Peter. *Chronicle of The Pharaohs*. London: Thames & Hudson, 1994. Print

Cline, H. Eric & Rubalcaba, Jill. *The Ancient Egyptian World*. New York: Oxford University Press, 2015.Print

Cooney, Kara. *"Queens of Egypt: When Women Ruled the world."* National Geographic Partners, LLC. Washington, DC. October 2018. Print Society, October 2018. Print

*Empires: Egypt's Golden Empire*. Direct. Ciara Byrne & James Hawes. Perf. Keith David. Empires Special, 2001. PBS. Documentary. May 2019.

Gahlin, Lucia & Oakes, Lorna. *Ancient Egypt: An Illustrated Reference to The Myths, Religion, Pyramids, and Temples of the Land of The Land of The Pharaohs*. Pennsylvania Hermes House, 2002. Print

Hawass, Zahi (2010). *"King Tut's Family Secrets"*. Official Journal of The National Geographic Society, September 2010. Vol. 218. NO.3. Print.

Heath, Julian. *Archaeology Hotspot Egypt: Unearthing the Past for Armchair Archaeologists*. Maryland: Rowman & Littlefield, 2015.

Hoffmeier, K. James. *The First God*. Aeon Essay, 12 Feb. 2019. https://www.aeon.co. June 2020

Hoffmeier, K. James. *Akhenaten and the Origins of Monotheism*. New York; Oxford University Press, 2015. Print

Hornung, Erik. *Akhenaten and the Religion of Light*. Ithaca and London: Cornell University Press, 1995. Print

*In Search of History: Akhenaten- Egypt's Heretic King*. Direct. Gary Foreman and Frank Haney. Perf. Dan Ackroyd. History Channel. Documentary. 1997

Kemp, Barry. *The City of Akhetaten and Nefertiti: Amarna and It's People*. London: Thames & Hudson, 2012.Print

Madden, April. *"Book of Ancient Egypt."* London: Future Publishing Ltd, 2017. Print.

Mark, J.Joshua. *Ancient Egyptian Art*. Ancient History Encyclopedia, 26 May 2017. https://www.ancient.eu May 2020

McMahan, Ian. *Secrets of The Pharaohs*. New York: Avon Books, INC.1998.

McLaughlin, Elsie. *The Art of the Amarna Period*. Ancient History Encyclopedia, 22 Sept. 2017. https://www.ancient.eu.May 2020

Naunton, Chris. *Searching for The Lost Tombs of Egypt*. London: Thames & Hudson, 2018.

Reeves, Nicholas. *Akhenaten Egypt's False Prophet*. New York: Thames & Hudson, 2001.

Rubalcaba, Jill. *Ancient Egypt: Archaeology Unlocks the Secrets of Egypt's Past*. National Geographic Society, 2007.

Shaw, J. Garry. *The Pharaoh: Life at Court and on Campaign*. London: Thames and Hudson, 2012. May 2019.

Strudwick, Helen. *The Encyclopedia of Ancient Egypt*. New York: Metro Books, 2006.

Thomas, Susanna. *Leaders of Ancient Egypt. Akhenaten and Tutankhamun: The Religious Revolution*. New York: The Rosen Publishing Group, Inc, 2003.

Tyldesley, Joyce. *Chronicle of the Queens of Egypt*. London: Thames & Hudson, 2006.

Tyldesley, Joyce. *The Pharaohs*. Great Britain: Quercus Editions, 2009.

Wilkinson, Toby. *Lives of The Ancient Egyptians*. London: Thames and Hudson, 2007.

Wilkinson, Toby. *The Rise and Fall of Ancient Egypt*. New York: Random House, Inc, 2010.

# Photo References

**Rosicrucian Egyptian Museum (REM)** located in San Jose, CA.

**Pixabay**: **1 Million + Stunning Free Images to Use Everywhere.** https://pixaby.com

**Category: Images-Wikimedia Commons.** https://commons.wikimedia.org >wiki>Category: Images

TRAVIS "T.J." FRANK has always been fascinated by history; however, when he learned about Akhenaten and Egypt, did his passion for history come to be. He has a BA in History and spends his time learning about history. He currently lives in California.

Printed in Dunstable, United Kingdom